T0160196

RISE

AMAECHI OFOMATA

AN ENTREPRENEUR'S JOURNEY OF
STRUGGLE, SUCCESS, AND SIGNIFICANCE

Advantage®

Copyright © 2020 by Amaechi Ofomata.

All rights reserved. No part of this book may be used or reproduced in any manner whatsoever without prior written consent of the author, except as provided by the United States of America copyright law.

Published by Advantage, Charleston, South Carolina.
Member of Advantage Media Group.

ADVANTAGE is a registered trademark, and the Advantage colophon is a trademark of Advantage Media Group, Inc.

Printed in the United States of America.

10 9 8 7 6 5 4 3 2 1

ISBN: 978-1-64225-188-3
LCCN: 2020902224

Book design by Carly Blake.

This publication is designed to provide accurate and authoritative information in regard to the subject matter covered. It is sold with the understanding that the publisher is not engaged in rendering legal, accounting, or other professional services. If legal advice or other expert assistance is required, the services of a competent professional person should be sought.

Advantage Media Group is proud to be a part of the Tree Neutral® program. Tree Neutral offsets the number of trees consumed in the production and printing of this book by taking proactive steps such as planting trees in direct proportion to the number of trees used to print books. To learn more about Tree Neutral, please visit **www.treeneutral.com**.

Advantage Media Group is a publisher of business, self-improvement, and professional development books and online learning. We help entrepreneurs, business leaders, and professionals share their Stories, Passion, and Knowledge to help others Learn & Grow. Do you have a manuscript or book idea that you would like us to consider for publishing? Please visit **advantagefamily.com** or call **1.866.775.1696**.

To my mother, Beatrice. Her guidance was
instrumental in shaping my value system.

I also have to thank everyone who has made
my entrepreneurial journey meaningful.
My life is a testimony that anything is possible.

CONTENTS

FOREWORD

maechi Ofomata is a venerable giant in entrepreneurship, enlightening us on the core values of success, namely quality, integrity, and passion, which he adopted as early as the age of seven years. His book *RISE* is a treasure for aspiring entrepreneurs, as well as their parents, teachers, counselors, mentors, and friends. This book integrates insights regarding the social and emotional characteristics of entrepreneurial achievers with existential consciousness. In this book, Amaechi demonstrates a rare quality of making complex concepts simple and accessible to all readers irrespective of academic standing. Very deeply thought out concepts are presented in the most simple and easy to follow language.

Motivational speakers and teachers alike will find this book a gold mine of effective strategies to develop effective and achievement-oriented domains. Established entrepreneurs will discover themselves in the pages of this compendium of practical tips. Anyone interested in cultivating effective entrepreneurial skills will be delighted by the content of *RISE*. Asynchrony, perfectionism, moral courage, sensitivity, empathy, reflective thinking, tranquility, balance, and meaning are all explored in this book. The book is a carefully packaged detail, if you like, a story of hope, determination, and prosperity set in the unstable landscape of Nigeria and of the possibilities that exist for anyone who would like to experience success. It is the story of transformation from a state of want to abundance, affliction to affluence.

Young Marcel (as he was known for most of his life) was born into want caused by the despair and despondency of the challenging years of the end of the Nigerian civil war. However, he achieved very rare success in transforming himself from fetcher of water and hewer of wood to CEO of a conglomerate of organizations offering employment to many in the country. He has over fifteen years of practical entrepreneurship, managerial, leadership, and mentorship experience, resulting in his current status as founder and CEO of Africa's leading asset financing company, Amaecom Global Limited, which has branches across Africa and the Middle East. Its trademarked BuyNow PayLater™ model of asset acquisition has transformed the lives of thousands of Nigerians. What's more, Amaecom was named as one of Nigeria's top fifty professional brands in 2018. Amaechi's current mission is identifying budding entrepreneurs and catalyzing their journey to their destination. This mission is one of the reasons for the establishment of a business school and the compilation of this treatise on entrepreneurial wisdom.

The book comes in ten carefully packaged chapters. Chapter 1 introduces the focus of the book. Here, he discusses the rare and untold story of Nigeria as he lived it: the story of innovation, inspiration, work ethic, opportunities for local and foreign partners, and beauty of Nigeria and its people. He also discusses the challenging landscape. In Chapter 2, he presents the natural entrepreneur in the context of a new Nigeria with unfolding opportunities and the values of industry, community, education, and integrity. He closes this chapter with a careful reflection that would engender ameliorative actions. No wonder in Chapters 3 to 6 he elucidates various developmental epochs from early steps through starting over to scaling up and expansion. He elaborates on the peculiar traits and cultures that characterize each epoch as well as the demands on personalities. In Chapter 7 he discusses the process of getting into the business of property development, while in Chapters 8 and 9 he discusses very unusual topics like giving back and new frontiers. In discussing giving back, he enumerates the various efforts to plow back into the society that has given to him benevolently. Like an ardent believer in biblical teachings he demonstrates his understanding of Malachy 3:10, sowing back in remembrance of the God that gave him power to accomplish (Deuteronomy 8:18). Finally, in Chapter 10 he enunciates four valuable life lessons that are germane to the realization of the entrepreneurial dreams of the younger generation.

Entrepreneurial individuals can make a difference in Nigeria and indeed in the world currently in search for new development paradigms. This book provides a navigable pathway to our development destination. It exemplifies the critical role of empathy and compassion when they are channeled into a life of stewardship for global good.

BENJAMIN CHUKWUMA OZUMBA

Professor of Obstetrics and Gynecology,
Vice Chancellor, University of Nigeria, Nsukka

A WORD FROM THE AUTHOR

t is gratifying to stand on the first-floor balcony of my well-furnished, fully automated house in the nation's capital of Abuja and look back over the years recounted in the pages of this book. It has been a long but rewarding journey from my childhood helping my mother cut palm leaves in a tiny village in Nigeria, to sleeping on the shop floor of my brother's small motorcycle shop in Eket, to owning a multimillion-dollar asset acquisition company that owes its success to innovation, and to establishing a foundation that encourages young talent in Nigeria.

This book is my story from a small village in post–civil war Nigeria, where, as a child, I rose before dawn and walked for an hour with a clay jug to get water for the day. My mother, whom we will meet in the coming pages, ran two small businesses from our home. Her story is an example of the Nigerian people's ability to rise from poverty to financial independence. Her influence laid part of the foundation for my success, which is based on the core values of quality, integrity, and passion, which I began to adopt as early as a seven-year-old.

The story of Nigeria, as I lived it, is rarely told, which is why I have set out here to show you, the reader, the innovation, inspiration, work ethic, opportunities, and beauty of Nigeria and its people. Nigeria has changed substantially in the last few decades, and this is my opportunity to tell a different story—a story of hope and determination and prosperity set in the ever-changing landscape of my country and the possibilities that exist for anyone who would like to experience a Nigerian success story like my own.

When I started out, I had the benefit of being part of a wave across Africa called "Africa Rising," which referred to the rapid economic growth in sub-Saharan Africa after the millennium. Since the civil war, aside from having the seventh-largest population in the world, Nigeria had seen decades of comparative peace, increased consumer spending, and a growing sophistication in information technology. I wanted my work in Nigeria to represent more than just economics and business success. I wanted to draw on the African values of ambition, openness, hope, and respect. I believed creativity, drive, and imagination were vital to Africa's future. However, I wanted to be able to serve the need among Nigeria's lower and middle classes to acquire alternative sources of finance to afford the small comforts they needed to live a better life. I attribute my desire to meet the people's needs as the driving force behind my success.

Meeting the need of the people led me over the years to first sell motorcycles on credit as a small venture that incurred risks and failures. However, the lessons I learned helped me develop my BuyNow PayLater™ model of asset acquisition, which offered minimal risk and a steady return. This model allowed Amaecom to go from selling motorcycles to selling generators, refrigerators, water filters, and mattresses—items in great demand in Nigeria. Later, we began to manufacture these same products, which took branding and quality to a whole new level in the Nigerian market.

I wanted Amaecom to become the leading global grassroots one-stop asset financing company in Africa. In doing so, I wanted to enhance quality of life for people through the provision of unbeatable, stress-free asset acquisition solutions. This meant imbuing my core values of quality, integrity, and passion in Amaecom staff and then changing how we provided essentials to the people of Nigeria.

In due course, we expanded from retail and manufacturing into education, scholarships, and mentorship. My experiences in trying to find qualified people to work in my company, as well as helping young entrepreneurs get a start so that they could contribute to the Nigerian economy, motivated me to set up a business school to teach young people how to grow their knowledge and wealth and inspire them to take the leap and invest in themselves and in Nigeria. I set up a mentorship program to create a hub for young people to learn about business. I have also spent many years working with the government and banking system to make Nigeria more business- and foreign-investment friendly. Nigeria has a strong middle class and a burgeoning young generation. Whenever the middle class is strong, we have a very strong economy.

One of the most important lessons I have learned in my career and in my life is that there is always a way. If you doubt you can do something, stop doubting. You can do it. When you follow my story, you'll find that your greatest success will, ironically, not come from trying to generate the highest return on investment or the biggest profits; it will come by adding value to the lives of the people. Everything I have done from my earliest years, from my first job cutting palm leaves and making chin-chin, was to add value to the lives of people. The best advice I can give is this: be authentic, work hard, don't be afraid to fail. That is the lesson of my book. To my fellow Nigerians: take pride in Nigeria and its diversity and strength, and above all, treat people with love and respect. All of this you will receive back tenfold.

I am telling this story now to tell the story of Nigeria that people rarely hear. If people are open to learning and willing to work, they can make a great impact here. There are still many areas waiting for someone with vision and transparency to make a mark as I have done in my own small way.

The fundamental principle driving me has been to meet the needs of the people, to identify where they are struggling and to use the private sector to provide solutions the government could not. However, it is also important that the government continue to foster business and foreign investment in effective ways. I hope my story, as told in the following pages, will both inspire entrepreneurs to take a chance on Nigeria and motivate the government to streamline its policies to encourage investment and even involve entrepreneurs in the policy-making process.

I hope my book will make people feel the pride I have in Nigeria. I hope it will encourage people who believe in our brand and our goal to leave a legacy of quality, respect, and transparency to invest in our economy and in my company.

To all the people who appear in these pages and to everyone else who helped make this journey possible, I am eternally grateful.

CHAPTER 1

Nigerian Background

This book is my story, which starts in a small village in post–civil war Nigeria, where, as a child, I rose before dawn to walk for an hour with a clay jug to get water for the day from Lake Nanka, the nearest source of drinking water. The path was treacherous and the stream was deep beneath the earth. As a child, my most important job was to get that water below ground and to not break my mother's clay pot. After another hour-long walk home, I would do my morning chores before going to school. The story outlined in the following pages, however, ends in a very different way. It ends with me owning a chain of businesses across the globe.

Nigeria still suffers somewhat from the stigma of war, crime, and poverty. In the last few decades, however, the country has changed substantially. This book is my opportunity to tell a different story, a story rarely told about Nigeria, a story of hope and determination and prosperity set in the ever-changing landscape of my country.

Nigeria in Recent History

The Biafran Civil War in Nigeria, which started in 1967, was Africa's bloodiest postindependence conflict. It began with the January 15, 1966, coup, which was headed predominantly by soldiers of Igbo extraction of the eastern region, killing top politicians of northern extraction when compared to their southern and eastern counterparts. Thus it was perceived as an Igbo coup. By June 1966, there was a counter coup targeting military officers and civilians of Igbo origin. This was followed by a series of pogroms in Northern Nigeria massacring the Igbos—my tribe—prompting tens of thousands of them to flee to the east where the Igbo ethnic group was dominant. A year later, fearing threats to the security of Igbos and to the economy, Lieutenant Colonel Odemegwu Ojukwu and other representatives established the Republic of Biafra, comprising several eastern states after the peace deal at Aburi fell through. War broke out with the Nigerian government, and after some initial successful battles, the Biafrans were outnumbered and overpowered. Biafran oil fields, the Republic's main source of revenue, were confiscated, which left it too poor to import food. Over the next three years, over one million Biafrans died of malnutrition before losing the provincial capital of Owerri to Nigerian forces. Six days later, the short-lived Republic of Biafra surrendered on January 13, 1970, and the war was over.

The Biafran War, which ended in 1970, had an enormous economic impact on Nigeria, especially the southeastern region. It was not only about the loss of lives, but about poor health, and about lost means of livelihood and lack of infrastructure. After the war, the government gave everyone £20 (about $45) to rebuild their lives. It was a paltry compensation for the loss of their homes and money in the war. Two years later, in 1972, I was born into a region where people were only starting to recover from poverty and starvation. Nevertheless, it was a time of hope when people believed persistence, integrity, and hard work could pay off, and it did. Over the next five decades, Nigerian GDP per capita went from a record low of $1,089 in 1968 to $2,456 in 2016.[1]

There were good reasons why Nigeria achieved this level of growth and success. They say that necessity is the mother of invention, and this was true in the southeast of Nigeria after the war. People began to reassess and think outside the box. In times like these, innovations emerge. The strength and independence inherent in the Nigerian psyche brought people from economic disadvantage to financial independence. We became financially stronger as individuals and as a community.

We started over with almost nothing, which meant it took blood and sweat to get back on our feet. Men made a personal resolution to succeed. They drove trucks or worked as houseboys just to try to raise capital to do better. This instilled in me during my early childhood a sense of self-worth and mutual respect for my fellow countrymen.

After the civil war, many Igbo migrated to different parts of the country and the world. This allowed us to interact with different cultures and form affiliations with different communities. We were able to build strong partnerships based on trust and integrity.

Opportunities for Foreign Partnerships

Partnering with nationals has been attractive to foreign investors in part because of Nigerians' strong sense of integrity, desire for a better life, and hospitable nature. Nigerians are engaging and love interacting

---

1   "Nigeria GDP per Capita," Trading Economic, accessed November 2018, https://tradingeconomics.com/nigeria/gdp-per-capita.

with other cultures. We have traveled far and wide. We also love new things and new challenges. We care about our neighbors and about the well-being of others. The importance of other people became apparent to me early on when I learned that no one succeeds alone.

Today, this has translated into an ability to partner successfully with foreigners. The Southeast, once battered by war, has now become a business hub in part due to Nigerians' ability to form lucrative partnerships and foster a fertile ground for foreign investors. For example, multinationals such as UAC and Leventis have done very well in Nigeria over the years and have helped to bring rapid development to the country.

On a national level, these values and characteristics evolved not only into successful business dealings with foreign investors but also manifested in a corporate social responsibility and a desire to add value. People from all over the world have come to invest here. Many have become naturalized, brought their families here, and still live a good life here. I have friends from Lebanon, Syria, India, and the US. Many of them will say, "This is where we belong."

Muhammad Fouani, a friend and business partner who is the only authorized distributor of LG Electronics in West Africa, is from Lebanon but has lived in Nigeria and raised a family here over the last thirty years. I have another friend from Syria, Chief T. A. Tann, who founded his company, Alibert Furniture, in Nigeria in 1974. Today, his company employs over five hundred Nigerians. Since 1974, he has expanded his business across West Africa, and it is one of the leading furniture companies in the region. These are only two of the thousands of investors who have come to Nigeria to do business and made it their home. Part of this is due to the integrity and hospitality of Nigerians, which makes doing business here pleasant as well as profitable.

Another advantage Nigeria offers foreign investors is oil. Nigeria is one of the largest oil producers in Africa. Oil was discovered in 1958, and, by the time I was born, it dominated the economy. This had positive and negative consequences. With government revenue largely coming from oil, there was less focus on taxation. This meant one could build his/her own business, thus allowing small businesses and cottage industries to flourish as a result.

In addition to oil, we have enormous resources of coal, tin, and iron ore, which offer great investment opportunities. The agricultural sector produces groundnuts, palm oil, cocoa, and coconut. The country also has a booming leather and textile trade.

The Changing Landscape of Nigeria

Today, the Nigerian consumer market is substantial. The country's population was more than 185 million in 2016, 75 percent of which is under thirty years old. This makes Nigeria the most populated country in Africa, the eighth-largest population in the world, and the main driver in the African consumer market.[2]

Admittedly, Nigeria's political scene has a checkered history. When Nigeria returned to a multiparty democracy in 1999, the then-president Olusegun Obasanjo had the task of rejuvenating the economy. He pursued this through the National Economic Empowerment and Development Strategy (NEEDS) program, which focused on improving the macroeconomic environment, structural reforms, management of public expenditure, and pursuit of institutional and governance reforms. This in turn brought about streamlined administration and less bureaucracy, creating a favorable climate for business and industry, fostering a free market economy and privatizing oil service

---

2   "Nigeria: Population, total," The World Bank, accessed November 2018, https://data.worldbank.org/indicator/SP.POP.TOTL?locations=NG.

and petrochemical companies. It also offered investment incentives to stimulate private-sector investment, reform tax laws, and provide tax relief to encourage new investment. For example, the government grants a five-year tax holiday to companies interested in investing in difficult sectors of the economy to boost jobs and economic growth by allowing profits to be plowed back into the business.[3]

In 2004, an overhaul of the banking sector began, first with a reduction in the number of banks doing business and an increase in a bank's minimal capital requirement to operate. This increased the competitiveness of retail, corporate, and internet banking.

In terms of infrastructure—transportation, communications, electricity, and water supply—extensive repairs and new construction have been underway in recent years. Aviation has expanded to include four international airports and a number of domestic private Nigerian carriers. In addition, the telecom market is booming. Companies such as South Africa's MTN Group, a multinational mobile communications company, which operates in twenty countries, generates one-third of its revenue from Nigeria alone.[4]

All of these factors contributed to the 2011 analysis of Citigroup that predicted that Nigeria will be the sixth-largest economy in the world by 2050.[5]

---

3   Bassey Udo, "Nigerian Govt. Issues New Tax Holiday Guidelines for Investors," *Premium Times Nigeria,* August 7, 2017, https://www.premiumtimesng.com/business/business-news/239446-nigerian-govt-issues-new-tax-holiday-guidelines-investors.html.

4   "MTN Settles Nigeria Fine & Looks at Listing on the Nigerian Stock Exchange." African Business Central. June 11, 2016. http://www.africanbusinesscentral.com/2016/06/11/mtn-settles-nigeria-fine-looks-at-listing-on-the-nigerian-stock-exchange/.

5   "Global Economic Outlook and Growth Generators" Citi. n.d. http://www.citibank.com/transactionservices/home/sa/2011q1/cab/docs/presentations/day2_3_Economic_outlook.pdf

The Story of Nigeria

My story is an example of the kind of persistence and integrity that has brought Nigeria from the devastation of war to become the largest economy in Africa. My mother, whom we will meet in the coming chapters, was able to run two small businesses from our home. Her story is an example of Nigerian people's ability to rise from poverty to financial independence. The foundation for my success is based on core values that I began to adopt as early as seven years old.

In the following chapters, I will explore the changing landscape of Nigeria and reflect on my childhood growing up in poverty in a small village, moving to a small city to work with my brother, and beginning to learn the principles of entrepreneurship. I'll also look at how those early years imbued in me the core values of quality, integrity, and passion that I hold dear today.

My career trajectory was one of trial and error, upswings and downswings, and in the following pages, I'll tell my story—a real Nigerian success story—from my small corner of Africa.

CHAPTER 2

A Natural Entrepreneur

The year of my birth, 1972, was a time of recovery from the three-year Biafran Civil War that devastated Nigeria. It was a very hard time, especially for people from my part of the country in the East. My parents lived in the town of Gboko and married before the war. My father bought and sold a variety of items, including clothes and shoes, in the neighboring towns. This meant he traveled a lot. Two years after they were married, in the midst of the civil war, my brother Sunday was born, and they returned to my mother's village of Isuofia in the east.

Any money, assets, or property that people owned before the civil war was lost. After the war, the government gave everyone £20 (approximately $45) to start over and rebuild their lives. If they had a house worth a million pounds before the war, they were still only compensated with £20 sterling afterward. During the war, people left the cities and returned to their villages, but when they went back to the cities after the war, they found that their houses had been taken over by the indigenous tribe of that location. If an Igbo had a house in the western provinces, he returned to find it with new occupants who were not going to leave. To survive, my people had to be creative. They had to learn to create something new. This was my learning and experience from a very early age.

New Opportunities in a New Nigeria

By 1972, people were starting to recover. A lot of fathers were killed in the war. Families, especially children who lost parents in the war, were just trying to survive. That was how it was in my village. My father was not killed because he traded and brought supplies to the Igbo rather than fighting. However, when I was growing up, many people were still hoping that fathers and loved ones who had gone missing in the war would one day return.

By 1978, when I was six, people were adjusting to peacetime, working hard, and beginning to feel hopeful. At the break of dawn, the cock would crow and I would get up and go with adults from the neighborhood to fetch water from Lake Nanka, which was an hour's walk from our village and our only source of clean water. We would balance our clay pots on our heads. The path to the lake was treacherous, and it was very difficult not to fall and break the pot. Once we arrived home with the water, we did household chores, swept the pathways, and got ready for school.

During the day, I liked running errands for my parents because it meant riding my father's "Long John" bicycle. His bicycle was made for men; it had a long chassis that made it difficult to sit on the saddle and reach the pedals because of my size. I had to ride "monkey style," squeezing through the chassis, which meant I could pedal but couldn't stand up. Nevertheless, I liked riding all over Isuofia. At night, we played by moonlight in the village square and listened to stories being told by the elders.

Childhood was short in some villages in the eastern region. By the age of ten, boys had to leave home to work for a tradesman and learn a trade. They typically worked for six to ten years without pay, but at the end of this apprenticeship, the master would help the apprentice to set up his own business. At that point, the apprentice-turned-master picked another child who deserved a good life and took them on as an apprentice to run a shop for the next six to ten years without a salary. This tradition continues to play out for the uneducated classes.

My childhood ended even earlier than this. I loved learning, and my parents wanted me to have a bright future. The only option they had was to send me to live in the city with my aunt. At the age of six, I was sent to Sapele Town on the western side of the country to live with her. Leaving my family and my community at such a young age was hard. The city was far away. It had bright lights, and everything moved quickly. It was a melting pot of people from different tribes. It took me a lot of time to adjust.

I was working very hard. I was doing my aunt's household chores, selling seasonal fruit and vegetables on the street, and taking care of her newborn baby. This wasn't the life my parents wanted for me. They had sent me there to go to school.

Aunty sent Marcel to hawk wares before he was six years of age. He would run after potential customers and describe the benefits of using the wares he was selling. He devised ways to sell the wares quickly so that he can go and play football! He would go back to his aunt who would give him household chores to do. Marcel always liked life outside the home because it meant he would be free to be on his own rather than go home to being piled with house chores to do.

MAMA OFOMATA

Three years later, my aunt and I visited my village for Christmas. I was glad to be home to my parents and my family. When my aunt asked me to go back to the city, she expected me to jump into the car with them, but I took a stand. Even at ten years old, I knew my mind.

"No, I'm not going back to the city," I said. "I want to be with my parents." And so, at ten years old, I abandoned city life and stayed in Isuofia in rural eastern Nigeria.

My three years in Sapele Town might not have been what my parents hoped for me, but when I returned to village life, I discovered they benefited me in many ways. I had been exposed to different experiences and cultures, so I had a level of sophistication even at that age that I wouldn't have acquired had I stayed in the village. I developed an ability to sell products and the ability to speak what we call "pidgin" English. Nigerian pidgin is an English-based language that has become a creole language. All of the ethnic groups in Nigeria speak this language with their own variations, which makes it the informal *lingua franca* of Nigeria. However, unlike other creole languages, most speakers are not true native speakers, and children have to learn it at an early age. When I returned to my village, I was the only child in school who could speak it well. It helped my comprehension and my curiosity, which in turn helped me do well in school.

Learning the Value of Industry

My father was a caring man, but he was away most of the time. He was a trader in all sorts of businesses. During the civil war, he traveled from city to city with an old bag in which he kept his money. When I was ten, he gave me that old bag. I treasured it and carried it to school every day. In no time, it was nicknamed *Akpa nwa dibia,* which means the bag of the native doctor or the witchdoctor. In the bag of the witch doctor, there is everything he needs, and my bag had everything I needed—my books, my little treat for lunch. It wasn't beautiful, and it didn't look like much, but I didn't care. Of course, it wasn't a doctor's bag, but I guarded it closely.

At this time, my mother taught me to do things that other kids couldn't do, which made me useful around the house. I was always busy doing things for my mother. She worked at home but also ran a successful business. She was the first woman in our village to start making something that looked like a doughnut, called "chin-chin," or *Okpa*. She had to wake up every morning at three o'clock to go to the mill to mill the flour. I never found it boring. It was fun for me and never felt like work. I never had to be told twice to get up and help. I ended up keeping the house, doing many of the chores, and helping my mother. I took great pride in that. I was excited about life because I could make life easier for her.

When he was a child, he was a very smart child. When I was selling Okpa, he would wake up at three o'clock in the morning to make Okpa because it must be ready by six! He would assist me in preparing the Okpa. He would assist in grinding pepper. He would tie the smaller ones while Mama Ofomata would tie the bigger ones. I would go to the market and leave all the pots and utensils for him. Everywhere would be dirty pots, plates, and every other thing used in cooking. At this point, he would call other children to assist with the chores. He would usually call out, "Umazi bianu o." And the children would respond, "Yoo!"

MAMA OFOMATA

Umazi bianu o! was a way of inviting other children to come and help. We lived in a beautiful community where everyone would come and lend a hand when called on.

In our village, almost everyone kept animals. They depended on these animals, particularly goats, for a living, and these goats were fed mostly with the palm leaves. Palm trees also produced fruit that we could eat or sell, so the palm tree was key to the village economy. At ten years of age, I told my parents that I wanted to take care of our goats and sheep and help with the palm trees. First, I learned how to plant them, which none of the other kids knew how to do. Then, I asked my father to get me a rope so I could learn to climb the trees. After all my household chores, I would take the rope and climb the palm trees, first the smaller five-meter ones, but within a year, I was climbing trees over ten meters. Being able to do that for my family gave me a great sense of pride. The neighbors saw me working like this and would say things like, "He's very small, he could hurt himself!" I became good at climbing palm trees because it became fun.

Despite his small stature, he would bravely climb the oil palm tree and cut the palm kernel for me. This saved me from paying someone else two shillings to cut the palm fruits for me! Soon enough, I would talk to my friends about how my little boy was helping cut palm kernel. Soon they all started calling Marcel to cut palm kernel for them, and he would assist them all in cutting their palm kernel at a relatively cheaper rate. He made some considerable money from this, and the money, though little, helped in making life a bit easy for me.

MAMA OFOMATA

Soon the neighbors were giving me some money to cut palm leaves for them. It wasn't much, but at eleven years of age, it seemed like a small fortune. To maximize the time I had to earn this money, I started employing other children to do my household chores and paid them a few kobo, or pennies, out of the proceeds from my palm cutting. I gave some money to my mother and used some to buy clothes for school and church. In other words, I had become financially independent at the ripe old age of eleven.

Learning the Value of Community

I always looked up to my mother. She was always busy, but never too busy to teach me some skills. Influenced by her example, I gathered the children from my area and showed them how to do everything I did. It felt good to have people around me. I learned back then that I didn't want to walk alone. Even today, I believe that no one wants to be alone. I believe that we make it by coming together and being valued and valuing others. I saw that in the aftermath of the civil war, as well as in my childhood when I was separated and then reunited with my family and my community. This motivated me then and still does to progress by building a community. This evolved into one of my core values: you can't succeed alone; you need other people to succeed.

> YOU CAN'T SUCCEED ALONE; YOU NEED OTHER PEOPLE TO SUCCEED.

As a child I faced obvious challenges, but because I was so young, curious, industrious, and thrived on new opportunities to learn, I never perceived them as obstacles. However, that changed at the age of twelve when I decided that I wanted to be a priest.

Our local church was Catholic. I went to church, took Communion, and tried to be good. At my age at that time, people believed that good people went to church and bad people didn't. We looked up to the priests who looked saintly and lived in fancy houses and drove nice motorcycles or cars. I wanted to live the good life like them. Southeastern Nigeria was producing the highest number of priests at that time. Unfortunately, my family couldn't afford to send me to seminary. They needed me to go into business to help them.

Sunday, my brother and eldest sibling, was living in Eket, a city near the Gulf of Guinea, and because I was adventurous and enterprising, my parents thought it would be a good idea for me to work with him in his small shop. I cried about this for many nights, but I didn't know then that my brother would become one of the most inspiring and influential people in my life, not just as a responsible businessman, but also as a responsible citizen. Sunday was loved by everyone. He was the first son of the family of many children, and he took the family burden upon himself. He cared for everyone. He was dedicated to his job and taught me to look at everyone as my responsibility and to care for them, too.

I hadn't seen a lot of him or my two other elder siblings growing up. One lived with an uncle, one with my father sixty miles away in Port Harcourt, where he was working most of the time, and another lived with my grandmother. My younger siblings lived at home. It was common in those days for children to live with relatives in the extended family. After the Biafran Civil War, it was hard for a family in southeastern Nigeria to survive. No one owned property or cash anymore, except for the £20 handout from the government. Most men, especially those with little education, had to go to the city for work or to trade to survive. Most men left the villages for the cities, which meant the children had few male role models. Men who were traders usually lived in their shop and would come home at Christmas with whatever profit they had made during the year.

Because I couldn't go to seminary to become a priest, I was sent to live with my brother in Eket after I finished primary school. My brother had moved to the South to start a motorcycle business after his eight-year apprenticeship finished and he was given the money to open up his own business. Unfortunately, the money wasn't enough to rent a shop and open a business in Benin, the city in which he apprenticed, so he had to migrate to Eket, where rent was cheaper. Eket was also an oil-rich city, so there was a strong consumer market there.

Most migration happens in eastern Nigeria when a boy finds someone who is wealthy or who is doing very well with whom to apprentice. Then, at the end of the apprenticeship, the apprentice may not be able to compete with the master in that location. To survive, he must go to another area that's less competitive to start out on his own. One skill of the Igbo is an ability to recognize where there is demand and then move to that area to build our lives. If someone is doing well, he'll bring someone who is close to him, a young person, to apprentice with him for eight years in order to learn the trade. This tradition is perpetuated from one sibling to the next and from one generation to the next.

Although I didn't want that life, I ended up working in Eket with my older brother. He didn't want me to be a priest. He wanted me to go to secondary school, so I started attending Government Secondary School Eket, while attending St. Gregory Catholic Church, which had an Irish priest called Father James Sharkey. There weren't many people from my tribe in Eket at the time, and I felt lonely. Father Sharkey had been there for some time and knew the area. Because of my education, he asked me to be an altar boy and help him as he prepared to serve Mass in surrounding area. This meant fetching and carrying, ringing the altar bell for Communion, and a lot of travel. There was a decent network of roads around Eket at the time, but few bridges, so we often went by boat to other cities to serve Mass on Sunday. One such place was Ibeno, a small town that had no church. We'd arrive on shore and had to walk on the hot sand for hours to get to where we could serve Mass. We'd then walk back along the coast to our boat and row back to the city. Today, Ibeno is booming. It has huge churches and schools. I was delighted to see this and proud that I was one of the first people to serve Mass there.

The Value of Education

During my early urban experience living with my aunt, I formed my first core value: education. City life shifted something in me, and I continuously challenged myself to get a better education and become more knowledgeable. Teachers began to pay attention to me, and I was soon recognized as an exceptional student. In addition, because I'd lived in the city and mingled with different tribes, my peers saw me differently. I began to help them learn, mostly because I had a desire to be helpful. An old woman in my village even gave me money because I was so smart. Other kids started coming around, asking me to teach them Pidgin English and mathematics. At nine years of age, they were calling me "the professor." This was how people came to know me and like me. They saw me as an exceptional child. I felt good, confident. We were poor, but I lacked nothing. I saw everything in school, every chore, every skill as an adventure.

Marcel demonstrated unique qualities as a child. He would always gather the children around the village to play, and after play he would ensure he gave them something to eat.

MAMA OFOMATA

When I moved to Eket at twelve years old, Sunday was struggling to set up his motorcycle business. It eventually became successful, but at that time he couldn't afford a car. He rented a room outside the shop, and I lived in the shop. I would wake up in the morning, get the newspapers, and open up the shop. I made my breakfast in the back room and then walked thirty minutes to school. After school, I'd come back and help him in the shop. This went on for six years, over which time his business did better and better. By the time I finished secondary school and was admitted to university to study engineering, he was so prosperous that he could help to pay my fees. I was the first member of my family to go to college, and that made me proud.

The Nigerian construction industry was booming at the time. After seeing the destruction wrought on infrastructure by the civil war, I had an image in my mind of how the cities and towns could look if they were rebuilt. I wanted to fix the community. I was interested in building highways and buildings. I had great ambitions to make our homeland great.

Unfortunately, two years into my college degree, Sunday got sick and died. His passing was hard on us all because he was the light of the family. The family's flame of hope was extinguished, and despair took over. For our family it was our sun getting eclipsed and darkness looming. The grief and pain was unbearable for me, knowing what promise he held. He was emotional and spiritual. He was my hero. He gave me the foundation for my life; he gave me all the support he could. He believed in me and would have helped me reach any level I wanted to attain. The rest of my brothers didn't have his confidence, drive, and ability, which meant they couldn't continue what he started. I was heartbroken to lose him.

His business was doing well when he died, so my two other brothers came to live with me and be part of the business. We discussed who should run it. I was the obvious choice, but I wanted to stay at university. They wanted me to leave school, and when I refused, they made me choose between staying in the business and having them take care of me, or staying at university and being completely on my own.

In those days in our part of the world, people were often so poor that a child could only go to college with the help of the entire community. The community would come together and raise the money, selling their palm fruits or yams, to send one child to college. College was a collective, not individual, effort. Thankfully, times have changed. Then, however, without this support from my family and community, continuing at college was difficult. Nevertheless, I was adamant that I had to go to college even though nobody else in my family had gone.

My family didn't understand why I wanted to go to college. In our village and our socioeconomic class, it was normal to get a master/apprentice position, then go out and make money and come back home to show how well you were doing. Because of this, most parents wanted their children to learn a trade instead of going to school. Like Sunday, I saw things differently; I saw education as something I couldn't do without. My commitment to education was based on my experience of seeing educated people doing well. When I lived with my aunt, I saw that there were better opportunities for those who went to school, and I had seen how education had benefited Father Sharkey.

The Value of Integrity

While I was in secondary school, very few people in the community had cars. Motorcycles were a status symbol, and most of the teachers rode their own motorcycles. The principal of my secondary school, Mr. Udombang, even rode a Vespa. When they needed repairs, I told them to get their spare parts from my brother's shop. If they didn't have the money, I would tell my brother, "These are my teachers. They're going to pay you." I sourced the parts they needed, and he would sell them on credit. Because I helped them when they needed it, I ended up being on friendly terms with Mr. Udombang and most of the teachers. I could also ride my teacher's motorcycles, so even though I was young and small, I was seen as mature, intelligent, and destined to do well.

Sunday had a power bike, a Honda CD 195, which was the talk of the town. I "borrowed" it occasionally to get to school, which made me quite popular. That's how I met Tim Barker, a member of the Voluntary Service Overseas (VSO), who taught technical studies. We would ride our bikes to Ikot Abasi to see his friends. Ikot Abasi in those days was a bustling town with a lot of expatriates. Many of the expatriates were helicopter pilots who had power bikes and motorcycles. Naturally, I supplied them with bits of motorcycle spare parts and made some extra money on the side.

This early exposure to white people, particularly on a business level, made an impression on me. I learned I could do profitable business with them as long as I demonstrated integrity in business dealings. Integrity was the next core value I developed. The emphasis on integrity in business stayed with me throughout my secondary school days and in all my business dealings afterward.

Sometimes, when I had free time, I would go to a five-star hotel in Eket by myself, buy a Fanta, and watch how people dressed and moved around. People from my part of the city did not go there. The guests were mostly English people. One day, my brother saw me sitting in one corner drinking Fanta. He took me home and beat me thoroughly. I don't know what he thought I was doing there, perhaps he suspected I had a nefarious agenda, but I knew it was a very bad day for me.

IF SOMETHING WAS POSSIBLE FOR OTHER PEOPLE, IT WAS ALSO POSSIBLE FOR ME IF I JUST FIGURED OUT HOW TO MAKE IT HAPPEN.

I sat there because I wanted that life. That's where I wanted to be, and I decided that was where I belonged. I have always dreamed of excellence, and this was what I saw as excellence. However, from those times spent at the five-star hotel, I learned a valuable lesson: if something was possible for other people, it was also possible for me if I just figured out how to make it happen.

I knew that if I were ever going to achieve this way of life, I had to choose education over the family business that I'd helped to build with Sunday, my brother whom I greatly admired. It was a difficult choice, and it ushered in a difficult part of my life. I lost my brother. I lost the business. I lost my home. Without the means to pay for college, I lost my place. I was twenty years old and already I had to start my life over. However, I had seen how life could be, and I was determined to live that way.

ON REFLECTION

My early teenage years taught me that it didn't matter who anybody was or where they came from. It did not matter if you came from a poor background as long as you were clever enough to figure out how to get where others were. It was an interesting revelation to have at such a young age, and it testified to my belief that I wasn't excluded from anything. All I needed was commitment, ingenuity, and a willingness to work. I decided that no one had to be a victim to circumstances. Anyone can make their life happen the way they want it to be as long as they realize they have the power within to change their circumstances.

I had that power. I didn't know how I would change my circumstances, but I would find a way. In my early years, I also learned the power of association, the power of having mentors. I didn't know what "mentor" meant at the time, but I looked up to certain people from the start, especially Sunday. I admired the way he did things, and I tried to copy him. This led me into the next stage of my life as an entrepreneur striving for success in the changing landscape of Nigeria.

CHAPTER 3

Early Steps

L eaving home at a young age gave me a different perspective on what life could be, and, as I mentioned in the previous chapter, seeing different people grabbing different opportunities showed me that I could choose the kind of life I wanted to lead. As a child, I'd learned to hold a conversation with a mix of people who were doing well in life, and I recognized that a more fulfilling life awaited those who were educated, which is why I adopted education as a core value. When Sunday died, this road became even harder to follow for a poor village boy like me, but I was determined to find a way.

While my brothers took over Sunday's shop, I went out and found a smaller shop on Liverpool Road in Eket and set up a small motorcycle business with the little I'd saved and the experience I'd gained. It wasn't much to start out with, but my experience included knowing the importance of surrounding myself with the right people. I had learned a lesson as a teenager from working with Sunday that the people I spend time with and listen to will shape me. This led me away from people who were happy to just sit down and do nothing. I sought out innovative and industrious people whom I admired.

First Step: Appearances

My father died when I was in my third year in secondary school. Four years later, Sunday died and my mother was heartbroken. The loss took an emotional toll on her. Sorrow and despair filled her soul. She had been so proud of Sunday. I went back to our village and brought her to Eket to stay with me in my new shop. I was just beginning to rebuild my life and my shop was very small, a mere twelve-by-twelve feet, but my mother noticed something different about my setup.

I remember visiting Marcel once in Eket, and I noticed he divided his spare part shop into two. One part had goods, the other part was an office! I was wondering why he didn't use the entire space to keep his goods, and he insisted that there was a need to have an office space to ensure that his customers had a space conducive to discuss business with him!

MAMA OFOMATA

My mother laughed because I insisted on keeping one part of the office for books and for meetings. I arranged the place very nicely, although it wasn't normal at the time and people thought it strange. "Why do you have to waste this space to make an office for us to sit down?" she asked.

"I want some of my clients when they come to just have a comfortable office to meet with me in," I said.

"They can use the whole place," she replied.

"No," I said. "I would like to have an office separate from the shop."

I knew even then that appearance and professionalism would be key to growing my business. I took this a few steps further. I printed up business cards with that office address as my head office but added branches in the six state capitals of Nigeria. Of course, I had no branch offices, but even in my small shop in Eket, I had big dreams to take the business global. Looking back now, it was childish and maybe a little crazy, but that was my thought and vision for the future. I never knew how this would play out, but it did. Today, I have offices in all of those cities and more.

Back then, without Sunday for support, I was trying to work and pay my fees out of my office and shop. Because of my workload, I rarely got to spend time at college. I was either in my shop or traveling around the Southeast, buying parts and coming back to Eket to sell them. I missed so much class that I ended up having to drop out.

As disappointing as that was, my new business was doing well because I retained a good customer base from my time working with Sunday. In addition, old motorcycles were everywhere in Eket in those days. I started taking them apart and selling the parts in Nnewi, which is the second-largest commercial city in Anambra State in southeastern Nigeria. I had so many parts from old motorcycles that I began loading up a truck and driving to Nnewi to sell them. It was a lucrative line of business, so much so that I was able to buy my first car, a Datsun Sunny, when I was twenty-four years old, a remarkable feat for a young Igbo in southeastern Nigeria. With my Datsun, I could travel to and from Nnewi more easily to do business. Unfortunately, my competitors got the same idea, and my profit margins grew slim.

Second Step: Financial Responsibility

At this time, Mobil Producing Nigeria Unlimited (MPN) was one of the largest oil producers in Nigeria with a contract to drill Nigeria's oil reserves. I got a job as a contractor on its construction site for a few months. It paid better for fewer hours than those I was putting into traveling around and buying and selling spare motorcycle parts. At the time, I needed to earn more money if I were to pay for school. In the few months I worked there, I resolved to save and finish my education, whatever it took.

Working for Mobil presented new experiences. I learned how to manage people. The site was in a swampy area that flooded the ExxonMobil buildings and needed to be dammed. My team mixed cement with sand and filled bags, which we aligned and stacked one at a time to build a long wall around the waterfront. It was a big job, and it took a lot of bags to dam the water seeping up from the gulf. Since I had been studying engineering in college, I acted like an engineer even though I wasn't one. Nevertheless, my confidence helped me manage people better.

My shop in Eket was still operational, but barely. I hired relatives to run it, but I had little time to focus on it during my months with ExxonMobil. It didn't matter too much to me then because I was earning a lot of money on the construction site. By twenty-four years old, I was rich. At least I felt rich. I bought some land on which I planned to build a house. Other than that, I spent freely. I was living a grand life. I knew I needed to save to go back to college, but I had so much disposable income that I didn't know how to manage it properly. I was spending more than I was saving. I was going to clubs on weekends and traveling about when I could. I was living in all the ways I'd never been able to afford. Unfortunately, I had no mentors to teach me how to manage money, so when the contract ended and wasn't renewed, I was out of work with only a piece of land and no school fees saved to show for my time. This was when I realized the importance of financial responsibility.

My only hope for a source of income was to revitalize my motorcycle shop, which had suffered at the hands of the relatives I hired to manage it for me while I worked with ExxonMobil. I had to sell part of my land to get my business off its knees. Thankfully, developers had come to develop the area in which I'd bought my land and its value had increased enormously, but having to sell my land brought me low mentally. I had a dream to build a house on my own land, and having to sell half the land meant that dream was gone. Not only did I sell a portion of the land to raise capital to reinvigorate my business, I had to sell off my car to supplement it. Amid this tumultuous time, I had no one to talk to, and no family nearby that I could turn to. I realized that all my friends who'd been with me when things were good disappeared when they were bad. Nobody cared, nobody wanted to help, and I felt very, very lonely.

Third Step: Integrity

That stage of my life taught me that I would have to go it alone and start building a network with the right kind of people—like-minded, enterprising people who would help me grow. I learned that you need to stand for something. The people with whom you surround yourself need to value you and that for which you stand. It's important to surround yourself with positive people who can be trusted. In my case, this did not apply to my fair-weather friends or my relatives who ran my motorcycle spare parts business while I was working at ExxonMobil. Importantly, this stage of my life taught me the value of integrity.

Falling after attaining a certain high forced me to think about my life: I needed to go back to school, but I also needed to manage my motorcycle business well to pay my school fees. I wrote the joint admissions and matriculation board again, and the following year I gained admission to Abia State University, Uturu, to study accounting. This allowed me combine my business with my education. I attended as many classes as I could. In my business, I used my newfound knowledge to create a good accounting system. My teachers taught me the importance of mentorship and seeking help from people who had more knowledge. I hired an auditor to work with me, and he also became a mentor.

YOU NEED TO STAND FOR SOMETHING. THE PEOPLE WITH WHOM YOU SURROUND YOURSELF NEED TO VALUE YOU AND THAT FOR WHICH YOU STAND.

Every month, I looked over all my accounts. This was unusual for a small business owner in Eket. As mentioned in Chapter 1, the government was lax in terms of reviewing tax returns, and it wasn't customary for small shop owners to keep such detailed records, though that has changed.

"Why do you have to work this way?" my mother asked when she saw my record books organized on shelves and all the extra paperwork I was doing. "Just sit down and relax."

However, I had learned the hard way that organization was key to success. My experience at that time taught me the importance of being frugal. I wouldn't make the mistake of not knowing how to manage income against expenditure again. I knew that I needed to keep my records straight and manage my debt properly, and I knew that ultimately this was part of a professional corporate image.

I knew that I needed to look successful to be successful, and that meant having an office and business cards. I had always had and understood integrity, thanks to the inspiring people in my life—my father, mother, and brother—but integrity became enshrined in my business practice at this stage. Integrity speaks for your trustworthiness as a businessperson and in building lasting relationships; when you say something, you must mean it.

Image was a challenge for me. I didn't have the money for expensive suits or a car. I had to hire a private car to take me home on the rare occasion that I did go home because I was too ashamed to admit that I couldn't afford a car. I didn't want to hear the villagers whisper, "He used to own a car."

Over time, with a lot of effort, my motorcycle shop started doing well. One of the reasons for this is that suppliers and customers had more confidence in me because of my corporate image. They trusted me and sold me motorcycles on credit, which I sold on to customers. They trusted that my word was my bond, and this allowed me to build a good reputation.

Fourth Step: Resilience

My early career experience influenced my future decisions greatly. I went back to college, but changed from engineering to accounting so that I might better run my business and understand the business world. I realized the importance of responsibility and good management. Unfortunately, despite my commitment to attending lectures and getting my certificate, I couldn't attend as much as the other students because I had to work in my shop. I hired an assistant and delegated some responsibilities, but because of the problems created by my previous assistants, who were relatives, I couldn't leave everything to him. This meant I had to spend more time in the office.

With no car, I had to take public transportation to get from my small city to other places in the region to acquire the spare parts that were the backbone of my business. I had to transfer up to three times to get to a supplier. Most of the time, it took five or six hours to buy spare parts. I'd come back to my shop to sell them and then go to school when I could. Unfortunately, dividing my attention between business and schoolwork made both my business and my academics suffer. I eventually ended up with third-class honors in accounting, but it took so long that I was thirty years old by the time I finished. Nevertheless, I did get the third-level education I had resolved to get.

Fifth Step: Expansion

Moving from selling spare parts to selling whole motorcycles was a logical next step, but it was a little premature, a little overambitious, and far more complex than my experience and the local economy could support at that stage.

It didn't take long for the individuals who could afford motorcycles to acquire them. Once they did, the market dried up. I needed a new idea to increase sales, so I decided to sell to groups in a microfinance capital accumulation system, which was popular in Nigeria. It was called Osusu (thrift). In this system, for example, ten people could put five thousand naira into a pot and then one of the ten would take the whole fifty thousand naira at the end with the promise to put in five thousand naira in the next group meeting to continue the process. Money is put in the pot daily, weekly, or monthly until a thrift collector collects it, who is usually a male member of the community. This process continues with each member taking turns until everyone in the group has a chance to use the money. It's essentially an informal form of peer-to-peer microfinancing.

Osusu was used in many areas and for many products in Nigeria. People used this microfinancing system to buy building materials for their houses, pay school fees or finance their wedding ceremonies, or start up a new business. At that time, it hadn't been used in the motorcycle business, so I was doing something different from my competitors. None of them had ventured into microfinance capital accumulation to increase sales. Implementing the Osusu system for motorcycle purchase meant I could attract a wider body of customers than just the person who could afford to buy a motorcycle by themselves. This increased the demand for motorcycles as well as my profits.

In addition, due to my positive outlook and professional attitude, suppliers wanted to work with me. They saw me as different from my competitors.

"There's something special about him," they said. "He's not like the rest of the guys."

Soon, business was going so well that I was able to marry Chika, a woman I met when we were both still in school.

I first noticed Marcel when he was brought to our class by our teacher to teach us mathematics when I was in SS2, and he made an impression on me as a brilliant young gentleman who was always available to explain the difficult subject of mathematics to the younger students. He was a year ahead of me in the school, and he always seemed so brilliant. The teachers were very fond of him, and he was used as an example of how we should all be as a student.

He would talk to me occasionally after school fellowship, as he also attended the charismatic Catholic fellowship with

me ... he always told me I needed finish my studies and
pass my examinations at one sitting.

CHIKA OFOMATA

Chika had gone on to Akanu Ibiam Federal Polytechnic, Unwana, Afikpo, in Ebonyi state to study accounting. After graduation, she went for computer training in Owerri and was then called up to do her required youth service with the National Youth Service Corps (NYSC). This organization was set up in 1973 by the Nigerian government as a tool for the reconciliation, reconstruction, and rebuilding of the nation after the civil war. The aim was to involve Nigerian graduates in the development of the country and in the promotion of national unity.

When we met in school in Eket, she was a junior and I was a senior. I encouraged her studies whenever possible even after I graduated.

Marcel later passed out of the school, and I missed him a lot. As he was just a friend, life had to move on, and I concentrated on my studies. One day in school I was told I had a parcel from DHL. I was curious and everyone else was curious as to how a secondary school student would have a package specially delivered to them in school. More curious was the person who could have sent such a parcel ... On receiving the parcel, I quickly ran to a private place to open it only to see it was from Marcel Ofomata! The parcel contained a letter and some past examination papers! The letter just asked how I was and generally encouraged me to face my studies. Though he did not say anything about liking me, it was good to at least receive a letter from him.

CHIKA OFOMATA

My relationship with Chika matured over the years despite long periods of separation. Finally, she graduated and returned to Eket. I had some land and my business was doing well, so I told her I wanted to marry her. I still had half the land I'd originally bought, but I was able to build something very small on my own.

My family resisted because my older brother wasn't married. They said I was too young to get married. However, I decided that I had everything I needed and had no reason not to get married. I knew Chika was the right woman. She was a wonderful lady and hardworking. We were a good match. Eventually, despite my family's protests, we had a traditional wedding and set out in married life.

Marcel had put together a "four corner" house in Afaha Uqua Obok Idem. No light! No fence! No water! Water was fetched from the next compound. Only the parlor and a room were ready in the house when we moved in! We only had love and hope in a better future to guide us.

CHIKA OFOMATA

At the time, mobile technology was new in Nigeria and only gaining entrance into the market. Chika started selling SIM cards and refilling SIM cards, which was a new business. From there, she started buying and selling telephones, mobile phones, handsets, and accessories to individuals and businesses. She was smart, had sales experience, and wanted to work, and she did well with that shop in Eket.

Chika continued running and expanding this small business in Eket while I worked to build my motorcycle business. She expanded from one to four stalls in a large shopping mall, but on the whole, she was more interested in maintaining steady business than taking risks and expanding. Today, she has eight employees in Eket even though we live in Abuja. She goes back every month to check on the stalls and calls her employees daily to make sure the business is being managed well.

Chika never wanted to take much risk and was prepared not to grow much as a result. She wouldn't fall down, but she wouldn't go much farther either. She chose to have a comfortable place and shied away from taking big risks. She had good reasons for this. We had a son to care for, and my younger brother was working for her, so her decisions reflected her responsibility to the family.

One of the reasons why Chika's phone business did well was because she brought a lot of experience to the table, and she makes good decisions at the right time. She has an ability to gauge people and recognize if a client was reliable or not. She knows when to say yes and when to say no to potential clients. This kind of discernment helped her stay in business because she was able to make more informed decisions.

However, while Chika ran her business at a steady pace, I was off thinking big. She was happy to make a little money and have a little fun. I wanted to do something more and take my accomplishments to a higher level. If you want to do something great, if you have a vision, you are never content to be where you are. That was how I was. I wanted to get ahead, so I took greater risks. Of course, with risk comes reward, but also the possibility of failure. There were two outcomes in any decision I took: I fail and pick myself back up, or I advance and leave my contemporaries wondering, "What happened? How did he get there?"

I was always trying to stretch myself and take things up a notch so that my motorcycle business grew. For me, if I sold two motorcycles one week, I wanted to sell twenty a week the following month, and fifty a week by the end of the year. I tried to make this happen by reaching out to more people, by having a bigger buy-in with the suppliers.

My competitors were surprised by my success and wanted to know my secret. There was no magic formula. My success was simply due to ingenuity and hard work. Every day, including weekends, I traveled to find groups that were large enough to afford a motorcycle in the microfinancing system; only occasionally would I come upon a group that could afford multiple motorcycles.

Eventually, I branched out beyond the Osusu system and began to sell to groups on credit. This proved to be much more difficult than I'd anticipated. The supply chain was almost impossible to manage, and some groups were not able to keep up the payments and disintegrated. There were no formal agreements or collateral to fall back on. When customers defaulted on me, I ended up defaulting on my suppliers. The profits I'd made previously weren't enough to pay the outstanding debts.

Sixth Step: Overcoming Adversity

Defaulting eroded the reputation I'd fought hard to build. Suppliers began to see me as unreliable. I had poured whatever money I had left after the ExxonMobil contract ended into building my motorcycle business, and it crashed, leaving me with nothing. It was a terrible slump, made worse because now I had a wife and a son for whom I had to care. From the high of having a successful business and a new marriage and family, it was very hard to be brought so low. I went from being looked up to, to being despised because I was indebted and couldn't pay back. I owed so much it was as if everyone owned a piece of me. Life wasn't worth living this way. People who had liked and respected me now felt betrayed. I felt I had been making a difference in Eket. I had been popular there, but now I felt rejected. I knew I had to start life over.

The machine spare part business collapsed! The mental stress was enormous. Whenever my husband is stressed and depressed, he withdraws into himself. He doesn't lash out or anything like that, but you have to force him to talk. The creditors were looking for him everywhere! There was an occasion when someone came to block our car in church, as we had "eaten his money!" At this point, we were preoccupied with paying back what we owed. Another man told him that he would "kidnap his son if Marcel doesn't pay him his money!"

CHIKA OFOMATA

There was nothing else to do except leave Eket, where I had lived for years. I had a house there and my new family. I didn't want to leave Chika and my son to start again in Uyo, the nearest city, where I had never been.

I could have stayed there and gotten a job or gone back to the old way of doing business through selling spare parts or microfinancing whole motorcycles. This had kept me going, but it was never going to grow into a great success. I knew I would end up with a mediocre career and lifestyle. There was a need for drastic action; I needed to take a risk and do something new. I had taken a big risk with selling on credit and failed, but I couldn't let that stop me from trying again. I had to try something different. The only way to achieve success is to put a lot of energy behind a new venture.

Despite owning my house and having no rent or mortgage, and despite having a happy family, I wanted more. I needed a challenge. I needed to get back on my feet after the failure of my small business. In the end, I had no choice but to move to Uyo.

It became difficult to walk freely in Eket, as people would accost my husband to ask him to give them back their money. It was really bad, and it got to a point that my husband had to close the business in Eket and move to Uyo to explore other ways of making ends meet.

CHIKA OFOMATA

Not taking Chika and my son with me was hard, but it made things a little easier financially. Had they come to Uyo, I would have needed to rent a better house. By staying in Eket, Chika could live rent and mortgage free in the house we owned, and she could continue to run her own small telecom company. That company was doing well enough that we could have ticked over, but we would never have been rich, and I certainly wouldn't have been fulfilled just running that business in Chika's slow and steady way. Therefore, in the end, we decided that Chika would stay in Eket with our son and support herself with the telecom business, while I went off to Uyo to get a new business off the ground. Chika understood. After all, it was still common for fathers to leave families to earn a living elsewhere. She trusted my judgment to do what was best.

ON REFLECTION

Having the drive is important, but setting goals is equally important. In hindsight, I got some of the basics right: creating a good image and earning and maintaining the trust of my suppliers. However, at that time I was unable to mitigate the risk of extending credit so that when clients failed to meet their obligations to me, I couldn't pay my suppliers. Had I some kind of risk-assessment measure in place, maybe the effect would be cushioned in the short term until I could find a solution in the long term.

While I made an error of judgment in trusting my clients to pay their debts, I was never deterred from pursuing my dreams. Rather, I saw the need for constant evaluation and improving my business processes to ensure my business would survive. This required making tough decisions, one of which demanded I leave my family to seek a new beginning at Uyo.

Making tough choices is important for success. I also learned that, to be successful, I had to identify my weaknesses and compensate for these by partnering with more experienced people. I learned to see mistakes as mistakes and not as obstacles I couldn't overcome. I learned that innovation is the only way out of a hole, as well as the importance of first impressions. It's important to not only be trustworthy but also to be *seen* as trustworthy. Integrity is paramount. Ultimately, I learned to always maintain the hope that there is a way forward. My positive attitude, hope for a bright future, and persistence, was all I took with me to Uyo.

With my lessons learned, I packed my bags for the state capital, Uyo, in 2005. I left Chika to run the phone business and resolved to think about business differently now that I was starting over again. My turbulent life in Eket had come to an end. I'd had hopes and dreams, gains and losses. I'd gotten an education and lost my brother. I'd gotten married and started a new life. I created and lost my livelihood. It was tough, but I learned a lot from the experience. I no longer wanted to deal with suppliers; I wanted to deal with the manufacturers directly. I wanted to cut down on the amount of negotiation I was doing with middlemen. Every stage of doing business involves capital expenditure in one way or another. Every negotiation involves time, energy, and time away from the office. Every negotiation costs you something. If you succeed, great; if you fail, you've lost more than just a potential deal.

My arrival in Uyo was well timed. The first wave of Nigerian banking reforms was going into effect, and these were set to open up many new opportunities on the road ahead.

CHAPTER 4

Starting Over

fter I moved to Uyo 2005, business was affected by the first of a series of banking reforms that started in 2004. Banking reform in Nigeria was needed at the time and helped make a difference in how business was done in the country. It wasn't an easy transition, however.

Prior to 1952 there was no legislation governing banking in Nigeria. When British rule ended in 1946, the following six years saw twenty-one of twenty-five Nigerian banks fail. This prompted a banking ordinance to be enacted in 1952, which was further strengthened in 1958 with the Central Bank Ordinance, which strengthened Nigeria's bank regulatory system. The Central Bank of Nigeria was created and began full operations in 1959.[6]

In the 1970s, when I was still making chin-chin in our village for my mother, miles away in the major cities more financial institutions were being created, and the Nigerian government was taking on a

---

6   Central Bank of Nigeria, "History of CBN," accessed November 2018, https://www. cbn.gov.ng/AboutCBN/history.asp.

greater role in their regulation. The Indigenous Enterprises Promotion Decrees of 1972 and 1977 established a policy that gave the government significant ownership of portions of the economy. In the banking sector, this meant the government took ownership of 60 percent of the equity in expatriate banks operating in Nigeria, including First Bank, Union Bank, and United Bank of Africa, the latter of which I later worked at for a time. After 1979, privately held banks began to emerge again in Nigeria, but the federal government dominated banking until the introduction of the Structural Adjustment Program in 1986. This program was introduced to allow the Nigerian government to borrow from the International Monetary Fund (IMF). The IMF required the government to decrease its regulation and ownership in much of the economy. Bank licensing requirements were eased, which resulted in an increase in the number of banks operating in Nigeria from forty in 1985 to one hundred twenty in 1992.

By 2004, the government stepped in again with reforms that consolidated the banking industry into fewer, financially stronger banks. At the time, there were eighty-nine fragmented and weakly capitalized banks, most of which were private, family-owned institutions with a capital of US $10 million or less. The government raised the minimum capital of banks to twenty-five billion naira (US $173 million) from two billion naira (US $14 million). They were given only eighteen months to come up with this capital, which meant there were a lot of mergers so that the new entity could have combined capital to meet the requirement. At the end of the eighteen months, eighty-nine banks had merged into twenty-five better capitalized banks. Any banks that didn't meet the capital requirement had their licenses revoked.

It was in the middle of this turmoil that I arrived in Uyo.

A New Vision

Leaving home and arriving in Uyo was not a well-thought-out plan. I hadn't wanted to leave and didn't want to be there, but circumstances were such that it was the best place to start over. Uyo is the state capital of Akwa Ibom, an oil-producing state in Nigeria, and it is more than twice the size of Eket. Uyo had more potential than the smaller city of Eket. When the chips were down, I had to leave my family to provide for them. I had a wife and a son to take care of. I knew I had to make a better future for them. After the failure of my business in Eket, I also had to take the risk to prove myself and achieve the goals I had always believed I could achieve.

Marcel has nerves of steel under pressure. He has compassion for everyone around him, and it has been a privilege being his wife. He knows where he is going. He always says things that eventually come to pass. When he was just managing one small shop in Eket, he wrote on his letterhead, "Head Office—Lagos. Branches all over Nigeria." At the time, he was just selling motorcycle spare parts!

CHIKA OFOMATA

When I moved to Uyo in 2004, I had a relationship with a successful banker, Emmanuel Atai Ekpo, at United Bank for Africa (UBA). I met him when he came to Eket to market the bank's products. The bank didn't have a branch in Eket, so when Emmanuel came to our town, he would visit customers and businesses in the area. He asked me to open an account for my motorcycle business with his bank in Uyo, which I did. I was one of the people he regularly looked up, so over time we developed a good business relationship. He liked my positive energy and my ideas and took an interest in my motorcycle business. Today, he has resigned from the bank, but he remains a very good friend.

Emmanuel was working in the bank in Uyo, so I decided to leverage my relationship with him and his bank and use the new banking reforms to my advantage. While I didn't have a lot of money to deposit in the bank and the turnover in my account was very low, I had plenty of ideas. Despite my setback in Eket, I arrived with my usual entrepreneurial spirit. I set out to find business opportunities, and between my determination, resourcefulness, and head full of ideas, the bank saw my usefulness and decided to partner with me.

When I arrived in Uyo, I didn't have a place of my own to stay, but one of my friends, the best man at my wedding who was from my ethnic group, was living there. I went to stay at his house. When I got there, he told me he wanted to move back to Eket, so I said, "Hey, give me your office. Give me some time, and I'll get the money to pay you." He trusted me and handed me his keys to his tiny office at 167 Ikot Ekpene Road.

When my friend took all his belongings and handed me the keys to his office, all I had was an empty office, a pile of debt, the equivalent of $139 in my pocket, and my ideas and integrity. I couldn't even pay the rent on the shop until I sold something that I didn't have the money to buy in the first place. Nevertheless, I was filled with high hopes because I could see opportunities abounding in Uyo that other people couldn't see. I was excited and ready to explore what lay in store. It turned out I had arrived at just the right time.

Initially, I got a job with Standard Trust Bank in Uyo. While I was at the bank, I noticed the enormous challenges that people had to surmount before getting access to small loans to buy electronic gadgets. I wondered why the bank didn't make it easy for individuals with good employment history to get small loans to buy electronic gadgets and pay the loan back over some time.

I sold the idea to the bank and was put in charge of marketing the idea to prospective customers. However, the 2005 merger between Standard Trust Bank and United Bank for Africa, one of the biggest mergers in the history of Nigeria's capital markets, which made UBA one of Africa's largest financial institutions, caused so many changes that my product became redundant and, by extension, my position.

This setback, however, was only temporary. When I was in Eket, I brought people together in a group to purchase using the Osusu microfinance system. That was so innovative at that time that it set me apart from other businesses and made me an innovator in the bank's eyes. Emmanuel loved how I had created market share in Eket and wanted to see how I could replicate it in Uyo.

I quickly realized the two cities were very different. The business plan I had in Eket wouldn't work in Uyo. It was too difficult to put groups of city dwellers together to use microfinancing. I decided I would need to find a new customer, a corporate client, and work with them and their employees instead.

Managing without Capital

I wasn't discouraged. If anything, I was energetic. With a population of half a million or so—twice the size of Eket—Uyo had far more potential to find corporate clients with large workforces. I was ready and willing, so when opportunities to network and pitch my ideas came, I was in the right place and in the right frame of mind. I analyzed my ideas to see which were viable, and then made decisions quickly. Unfortunately, I had one major obstacle—I had no capital. I couldn't buy stock first to sell; I had to find another way to get the stock I needed. This meant I needed people to believe in me and trust me on my word. Unfortunately, I was new in town and knew only one or two people, so getting stock without capital was going to be a tall order.

> I WAS READY AND WILLING, SO WHEN OPPORTUNITIES TO NETWORK AND PITCH MY IDEAS CAME, I WAS IN THE RIGHT PLACE AND IN THE RIGHT FRAME OF MIND.

Uyo was the seat of the provincial government and had a large middle class. I knew I needed to target that market. The working class was struggling, and they wanted basic things in order to live comfortably. Unfortunately, for most of them, their salary didn't stretch to many of the products they needed. I was trying to figure out how to help them when I came up with the idea of selling goods to them with some equity contribution made up front and the rest payable in installments. To avoid a repeat of Eket with people defaulting on payments, I decided the safest way to structure these deals was to make the deal with their employer, have their employer deduct the payments from their salary, and then pay me directly. I knew if I could get a large enough up-front payment from the employer, I could go to my suppliers and buy on credit from them and then repay them in installments as I received payments from the employees via the corporate client.

Armed with this idea, all I had to do was convince an employer to give a man with an empty office, no stock, and no money a large down payment on a large order of motorcycles for their employees.

Another challenge was being new in town and needing to find ways to get meetings. I got up each day and went from police stations to government offices to corporate offices trying to convince them that I could do what I was proposing and that it would add value to their workforce. I was paddling hard underwater to look smooth and seamless on the surface, and it paid off. I got a lot of positive responses. I was encouraged in each meeting, and that propelled me into the next phase.

I set up my shop as Amaecom Global Limited at 167 Ikot Ekpene Road, Uyo. It was a small office in a prime area. I started out with three staff members, and I insisted that the staff dress "corporately" to project an image of a serious organization. We looked professional and trustworthy in our operations.

I told Emmanuel my ideas and my plans. I needed his buy-in. I told him I was there to stay, but I didn't tell him I was bankrupt. I didn't tell him I didn't have anywhere to sleep or to lay my head. I just focused on the fact that I was there to work hard and turn the demands of the Uyo economy to my advantage. I also asked him to let me know if he heard of any good opportunities that could use an innovative entrepreneur. When he reads this book and finds out how broke I was then, he's going to laugh!

The first deal I made was with the prison service, which was a government office. Most of these government organizations had cooperative societies, so I could sell to the cooperative of the Nigerian Prison Service.

A cooperative society is an association of individuals who come together with the objective of owning common property and promoting the economic interest of its members. The Nigerian Federal Cooperative Societies Act regulates cooperative societies. A cooperative can either be employee based, credit based, or business based. Cooperative societies are a powerful and effective tool for wealth creation and investment and offer immense opportunities in addition to having the capacity to reduce poverty, enhance job creation, encourage savings, reduce business risk, and improve national productivity.

Since motorcycles were as important a part of life in Uyo as they had been in Eket, I approached the prison office with a business proposition.

"Look," I said, "I can help you assist your employees to get what they want, especially motorcycles, and they can pay in a way that's convenient, if I have the guarantee from you, the employer, that every month they will pay me." This idea was much bigger than my Osusu idea in Eket, but a bigger city demanded bigger ideas. I knew I needed to be dealing in bigger numbers because these corporations had more money, and they could make large contributions to service the needs of their employees. I went into these meetings and offered my bank information so they could do a background check.

I arranged to supply motorcycles to the prison service employees and allowed them to pay over time. They liked my proposition and ordered fifty motorcycles from me. It was my first deal. It was a huge breakthrough for me. I never imagined it could go that well. The prison service gave me 50 percent of the total up front, which I deposited in my bank account. This made Emmanuel happy. His innovative customer was generating business, which also helped to boost his career.

With an order for twenty motorcycles and many more on the way, I wanted to cut out the middleman and go straight to the source. I started conversations with other dealers and asked a lot of questions. My competitors didn't suspect that I was trying to find out who their suppliers were. I discovered that the Indians in Lagos controlled the business of importing motorcycles from China. Armed with this information and the money I received from the prison service, I made the ten-hour drive to Lagos to find these suppliers.

Building a Supply Chain

Lagos is a city in the state of Lagos. The Lagos state government estimates the population of the greater metropolitan area is approximately sixteen million, which makes it a megacity and the most populous city on the African continent. It is also one of the fastest-growing cities in the world and is a major financial center in Africa, with one of the largest and busiest ports on the continent.

Once I got to Lagos, I did some research to locate the offices of major motorcycle dealers. Then, I showed up at their offices. I didn't know these people; in fact, I didn't know anyone at all in Lagos, but I wasn't afraid of reaching out. I knew once I did, making a deal would be possible. I just needed to look the part and be confident enough. I presented my proposal and explained that I was a big dealer in Uyo and needed a big supplier. I explained that I needed twenty motorcycles immediately but would need to bulk buy more later.

I was young, but they believed me. I had a document from the prison service showing they had already committed 50 percent of the retail cost and that the balance would be due upon delivery. When I showed them my bank balance, it legitimized me as a customer. However, I had structured the deal so that the 50 percent I had been paid by the prison service was equivalent to 70 percent of the wholesale price. This gave the suppliers the surety they needed that I would have the other 30 percent soon and that the balance owed would be paid. Additionally, they could meet my bank officer, who validated me, and they could visit my shop. In the end, they trusted me. They saw that we were helping each other. They were looking for a way to sell their products to bigger markets and to have more customer accounts. When I arrived to be one of those larger customers, it was perfect timing for both of us. There was a synergy there, and that deal was a new beginning for me.

I got the fifty motorcycles back to Uyo in cartons, so they had to be assembled. I got an engineer to begin fixing the motorcycles. For a small shop like mine, this was a huge amount of work. I was the new guy in town and all of a sudden I'm doing the biggest business. Anyone who passed by the shop saw it filled to capacity, so word got around that there was a new guy in town who must be very rich. That perception was critical to my business, because it created momentum. I took pictures of all our work and our stock so that when the motorcycles were assembled and sold, I hung the pictures in my shop to show people the kind of business we did, and the kind of capacity we had to generate sizable turnover. At that stage, it was all about image.

Expanding My Business Model

The bank at the time wanted to finance assets for people who had jobs. The Indian suppliers wanted to sell more motorcycles, but people didn't have the money to buy, so I came up with a second proposal. I arranged a structured deal with the bank: if I could get a customer to open an account at the bank and put 10 percent of their salary into that account each week, the bank would lend me the other 90 percent to buy the motorcycles. This appealed to the bank because it wanted more employed people to open accounts. I then went to the Indian supplier and got him to agree to supply more motorcycles.

For example, I spoke to one man with a paid job, and convinced him to leave his bank and open an account with UBA and make a 10 percent deposit against a new motorcycle. The bank financed the other 90 percent. This made it easy for him to get a motorcycle and possible for me to expand my business. It wasn't easy to get people who had been with one bank for a long time to move to a new one, but they had something to gain by moving. This model was working so well that I started replicating this business model in other cities, such as Bayelsa and Abia State, Cross River, Enugu, and Ebonyi. This also meant UBA was also getting new business in these places, so much so that the bank gave me my own office in the banking hall.

No matter how Marcel travels, he would still be home for the weekend. I was in the shop one day when I saw someone driving a brand-new car toward my shop. The car was a Honda Civic, and the driver looked familiar. Lo and behold, it was my husband! He stepped out of the car and handed me the key! The whole town of Eket was agog as a man bought a new car for his wife!

CHIKA OFOMATA

My success unfortunately attracted a lot of attention from competitors. A teller in a branch told a competitor how I was structuring the deals. It wasn't dishonest. The bank was always looking for more customers, so one employee went to a competitor and said, "Hey, why don't you do the business this guy's doing? He's making a lot of money." This competitor then went and poached the staff members I'd trained to work with me and offered them double what I was paying them. What could I do? My business wouldn't have been viable had I paid them double, but these employees were young and wanted more money. They left, and my business came to a standstill.

After working so hard, and making my vision a reality, this was shocking. It was like being hit below the belt, and there was nothing

I could do. It's not in my nature to engage in the politics and intrigue I saw around me. I wasn't a seasoned corporate owner. I was in my early thirties, younger than these people who were undermining me. Integrity that helped me get my business off the ground, but my openness and honesty with the bank employees and my own employees hurt me now.

Learning When to Delegate

In hindsight, this experience taught me that if you have a vision, it's very easy for other people to make it theirs and run with it. However, just because they copied an idea doesn't necessarily mean it will be easy for them to execute. Often a concept looks easy until it's time to be implemented, at which point the execution can go astray. This became evident during the banking reform, which I'll talk about shortly.

In response to my challenge, my focus shifted to ethics and to building a culture of excellence to develop a competitive edge. I decided to change whom I employed and how I did business. I dealt with the bank and key clients directly rather than allowing employees to do so. Learning what responsibilities not to delegate was as important as learning how to delegate. I learned that when expanding I needed to develop the relationships myself. I needed to make my own calls, and then limit the information I shared with other people. I needed to create my brand myself.

I rebuilt my business to the point where I had four employees operating as a team. I noticed that the bank employees all dressed in traditional Maitama attire on Fridays, so I implemented that idea in my business. On the last Friday of each month, we all dressed in our own traditional attire, so that we could see that we were representing different tribes and cultures in our office. We extended that to a red tie on Tuesdays or a T-shirt on Thursdays. We began celebrating each other's birthdays together. This culture has evolved to this day. I learned from this early stage that employees need something more than just a salary to be loyal--something to always look up to and a connection strong enough to make them love the brand.

I built a new, strong employee base. We had a smaller market share, but we had a sense of teamwork that helped to keep it all going.

KNOWING HOW TO EARN TRUST AND WHEN TO BE TRUSTING COMES WITH EXPERIENCE.

Each employee only knew what they needed to know, so that I was able to protect my vision and proprietary information.

It took some time to learn to delegate again after my experience of seeing employees to whom I'd taught everything leave me for a competitor who offered more money. For a long time, I took on the crucial roles and delegated everything else so we could expand. Knowing how to earn trust and when to be trusting comes with experience. However, when an employee earned trust, it fostered loyalty because they knew they were perceived as trustworthy, and this added to our strength.

Becoming Adaptable

Rebuilding my company as new banking reforms got underway became a tough challenge. The banks stopped offering many services, including the program I had set up between the bank, the bank's customers, the motorcycle distributors from India, and myself. I was told the bank could no longer sustain the project or this business. There was a new management, and there was nothing we could do about it. The business was gone without discussion or negotiation, and I was still paying off debts in Eket. Once again, I had to find a way to survive.

The banking reform and the resulting crisis became a turning point. I had to rethink my whole approach to business. I struggled to pay salaries and had invested all my money in marketing because I hadn't anticipated the banking reform or the collapse of my program. I was back to where I started, just me and my office. It took a year to get back on my feet. I was going from office to office trying to drum up business. Many companies were going out of business because of the banking reform. It was a very difficult time.

The people who poached my staff ended up going bankrupt. They never had a vision. They only cared about the money coming to them, not the relationships or the value they were adding to people's lives, so when the banking reform came they couldn't innovate to survive. Some of the staff members who left me for those competitors before the banking reform came back looking for work. I wouldn't rehire them. I wouldn't have been able to trust them again. They had betrayed me, and loyalty is a key component of my corporate ethic.

Through it all, I kept going. If I couldn't drive, I walked. Some days I went to fifty offices in a day. I was tired, but I kept going. I kept talking. I kept adjusting and redesigning my program. With the bank out of the game, I went back to the workers and to my original program of making the 50 percent down deal with the employers. I wrote to all of them, and we struck deals whereby the employer deducted the payments from their employees for motorcycles and paid me directly.

ON REFLECTION

I had taken some knocks on my entrepreneurial journey in only a few years. What kept me going was self-confidence and belief in what's possible. I could see that people had needs. I learned that survival in business is not about how much money or assets you have but about your ability to adapt to change, which is constant in life and in business.

But on the positive side, I was cutting out the middlemen in the supply chain and expanding the business. I also learned at this time the importance of having people around who are supportive of the entrepreneurial vision. Delegating is as necessary as forging partnerships, which means building trust is imperative. I am loyal and people see that. I am also open, and while some people took advantage of that, on the whole, it is a quality of which I am proud. I offered people gifts as an expression of gratitude. When you express gratitude, people want to do more, so a sense of gratitude is very helpful.

Admittedly, finding a balance between forming trusting partnerships and keeping proprietary information secret was a challenge. Divulging too much information gave my competitors an advantage, because when staff members left, they took this information with them to their new positions with those companies. An important lesson I learned at that stage was finding this balance.

I also realized I needed to stay abreast of the economic climate; for example, had I foreknowledge of the impact on the bank merger on my business, I would have positioned my company to weather that storm better than I did.

In short, this phase of my business career was challenging, but it taught me many lessons that would go on to serve me as I moved forward with confidence. I knew that if people had confidence in the entrepreneur's spirit, growth was inevitable.

CHAPTER 5

Scaling Up

egrouping after the banking reform was difficult. My competitors had poached my employees, and even though they went out of business and my former employees wanted their old jobs back, I couldn't take them. Loyalty and trust were and are core values of mine. I had no choice but to rebuild from the ground up. It was a trying time. I had to figure everything out as I went along, with nothing to rely on but my own innovation and instinct. I had to learn to design processes, including writing proposals and arranging meetings. Many times, I learned more by making mistakes. I learned by being open to criticism. I looked for opportunities to evolve, learn, and innovate more.

My experiences of helping to provide motorcycles to people who otherwise hadn't the means to buy them gave me a new perspective. I began to see that I had a higher calling that could manifest in how I did business. Since I was starting over, I decided to change my approach to business. I began looking at employment laws and responsibilities in order to create a positive working environment for new employees.

My mother said I always wanted to lead, but I always wanted to lead and not to rule. Nobody walks alone. I knew that people can achieve a lot when they pull together. I shared as much information as I could to make them feel part of the business, while keeping some proprietary information to myself for my own protection, so that company wouldn't suffer if anyone left.

As the rebuilding process continued, the more the potential for my company became apparent and we decided to scale up. Clients still had confidence in my company. They saw how I had changed the playing field by dealing with the Indians in Lagos directly. No other motorcycle dealers had taken this approach to business before. They were dealing with middlemen and individuals and selling one motorcycle at a time. I had my own experience of doing business like this, enough to know it wasn't the future, at least not for a business that wanted to grow.

Redesigning my corporate structure and imbuing it with my values encouraged me to expand again. I wanted a better life for my family and myself, and I was prepared to do whatever it took. There is often a thin line between success and failure. Sometimes, you can make a great impact by staying in when you want to get out. I'd been staying in since childhood, and I was about to do so again.

Creating a Brand

My experience at the bank showed me the importance of image and branding. I knew I needed a theme and an overall look for my business. I also recognized the importance of referrals and references and the appearance of success. I hung photos in the office from past meetings and accomplishments, which bolstered trust. The more I networked with groups to do business, the more emphasis I put on showing that my business had money and a professional corporate image. All my employees wore a suit and tie. They drove nice cars and spoke well. This might sound obvious to most readers, but many people in Nigeria were doing business dressed in casual clothes and sometimes without shoes. That was not our way.

Each morning, I sat with the team and identified what we wanted to achieve and who we wanted to meet. Drawing on my experience with the bank, we drafted letters for potential clients and specifically tailored proposals for different groups of employees within different organizations.

I started writing to the administrators, the Imperial Court and the bureaucrats who were concerned with implementing the right plans. Politicians made the political decisions but the bureaucrats laid the groundwork and presented the ideas, so that's where we focused. My team spent a lot of time writing to them, forging relationships, and explaining what we wanted to do and how we wanted to create a better life for their employees.

When we pitched proposals to employees, they usually organized a committee and arranged a meeting to ask us questions. We rehearsed how to act and deal with them and how to explain the way the supply chain worked in advance. We gathered references to offer them. After meeting with us, the employees went to their employer with a request to implement a plan of automatic salary deductions payable to my company in exchange for goods needed. Once that was set up, I traveled to Lagos or to other suppliers to get the products.

Every morning when my team met at the office, I stressed the need to speak to people's needs rather than adopting a hard sell. We would then drive from office to office with the attitude that said, "We can help you with this. If you make a 5 percent contribution, we can supply your workers with what they need."

Over time my team learned how to seal the deal, and my role changed from day-to-day pitch meetings with employees to taking the initial meeting with employers. After that meeting, the team took over. The transition became seamless and simple, which was necessary so that the system could run without me being present. Everyone had a specific role in the overall process, which meant I could delegate without running the risk of my team being poached by competitors and then losing business because of it.

Strange as it sounds, this differed from how my competitors were doing business. We were known by our dress code, by how we walked and talked. We met and strategized and knew how to talk to people's need. Our competitors didn't have a corporate setting or culture. They just woke up and went out and talk to people. They didn't plan and pitch proposals and follow up or train people in order to delegate tasks. The bosses held information tightly, which meant they had to oversee everything themselves, and this limited their capacity to grow in the changing political and economic structure of Nigeria.

Underpinning our actions as we rebranded were our three core values of quality, integrity, and passion. We wanted these values to be reflected and entrenched in our business processes, transactions and culture.

Passion for Quality

By 2008, we had expanded quickly and our growth spurt attracted competitors who began offering their own version of the BuyNow PayLater™ model. They reached out to our clients, offered my catalog, and opened stores to sell products. If we were to continue to perform better than our competitors, we needed to evolve and continue to differentiate ourselves.

Our values of quality, integrity, and passion set the service we offered apart, but we needed to do more. We needed to also set our products apart if we were to firmly establish market dominance. I needed to raise the standard of the products we were selling and make sure we were known for reliability of quality. We couldn't control this by going to the stockrooms of other manufacturers for goods. The only way to do this was to manufacture and offer products under the Amaecom brand.

> **I NEEDED TO RAISE THE STANDARD OF THE PRODUCTS WE WERE SELLING AND MAKE SURE WE WERE KNOWN FOR RELIABILITY OF QUALITY.**

I designed a logo that represented us as a company back in the days when I wore all the corporate hats, including that of the brand manager. Since the company was founded in 2004, the men had worn red ties and women wore a touch of red on Mondays, which was just for fun, a little bonding ritual, so I incorporated red into the logo design. I appreciated the importance of branding and the need to show ourselves to be unique. This focus wasn't common in SMEs in Nigeria at the time. When I sit back and look at what we spent on branding and brand guidelines today, I wonder how we managed in those early days at all.

I needed to do more than just design a brand image; I needed to populate our stores with branded products. We had been buying products from manufacturers, so our product list was composed of a hodgepodge of different brand names. Over time, however, I realized we needed to be able to ensure quality. Demand for our products had risen significantly, but I began to look at the products we were offering at the time. It wasn't easy for a customer to recognize levels of quality. Some brands, such as Sony, have an established reputation, but often in the Nigerian market, products are designed to look like Sony, yet when the customer gets home, they find it's an inferior product. I did not want our company to inadvertently add products of lower quality to the market.

When you put your own brand on a product you want to be able to say, "This is the best." We wanted our brand to be recognized as a quality product that people could trust. We wanted people to buy our refrigerators because they saw our name and said: "Hey, because it has your name, I'm going to try that." You don't want to let customers down with your own branded products, because if you do, you also damage your credibility.

The Value of Trust and Transparency (Integrity)

The installment plan structure that I implemented after the banking reforms worked well for ordinary working people within the prevailing economic system in Nigeria.

In the coming months, I met with groups of employees and presented my business model. I told them what was possible in terms of supplying motorcycles on my down payment and installment plan. They would go to their employer and ask for a certain amount to be deducted monthly to pay for their product. As soon as the employer did that and I had three or so payments in the bank, I would get the supplier to extend credit for the difference and give me the products in advance. Because these people didn't have any money, this was the only way my business approach could work and the only way they could get what they needed.

At the root of this model were the values of trust and commitment. Integrity made growth possible, and to show my integrity, I first assessed whether the employees would really benefit and whether their intentions were genuine. I explained that their employer had to make an equity contribution and that would be deducted over time from their salary, but to make sure they wouldn't default, as had happened before, I said, "You have to make the deduction three times, and when I see the deduction coming every time, then I will be sure that I can now give you the product." This meant they had invested some of their cash in the product before they received it and would therefore be less likely to default.

When the deductions were made and the money was in the bank, I never touched it. I could go to the suppliers and show that I had a certain amount of money in the bank to pay them and then promised the balance at a set point in time. By seeing my bank balance and understanding the process, the supplier was then confident that he would get his money. Once the supplier agreed to sell me the products on those terms, I was able to bring them to the people who needed them.

One challenge I faced when I started writing or meeting with different corporations and organizations to address this issue was their fear of being defrauded. Many people had proposed schemes to get loans or advances and had defaulted. There was an element of distrust with which I had to contend. These corporations were willing to help, but they needed to see integrity and authenticity. They also wanted something original, not the same pitches that had cost them before. That's what I was trying to bring them. I brought transparency to the table along with references and professionalism.

From my experiences at that stage, I learned the importance of trust, but also of having the right documentation in place. Even though I wasn't asking for collateral, there had to be some understanding in place that I could fall back on if anything happened.

Without a doubt, establishing trust is crucial to running a successful business in Nigeria. It is far more important than raising capital.

Capital had not been a problem for me because I was able to think of creative ways around that with credit and installment plans. Over time, I was able to put money in the bank and make sure payments were being made. This transparency made growth possible.

The Challenge of Ethnicity in Nigeria

Nigeria is a multicultural country, having over seven hundred ethnic groups. This comes with its attendant advantages as well as its challenges. One of these is the challenge of tribalism. While groups feel the pressure of globalization, tribalism is strong because it is founded upon intense feelings of common identity, which is why it is as powerful as religion in Africa. Tribes generally look to advance their own interests in the political system, and this often leads to discrimination against people from other tribes.

Tribalism controls how people think and talk and determines what they oppose or support. It is weaved into the fabric of Nigerian society and is passed from one generation to the next. This is why conflicts in Nigeria that are based on ethnic competition often get in the way of economic development.[7] Other countries are not as focused on their ethnic differences as Nigerians, and this makes embracing this diversity important for anyone who wants to be successful here.

The roots of tribalism go back a long way. Before independence, British colonial administrators based their policy on regional autonomy, which divided Nigeria along ethnic lines. After independence in 1960, the country remained dominated by tribes: the Yoruba in the west, the Igbos in the east, and the Hausa/Fulani in the north. Political parties were formed along these ethnic lines, and intertribal distrust

---

7   Chinua Achebe, *The Trouble with Nigeria*, (Enugu, Nigeria: Fourth Dimension Publishers, 2005): p. 17.

resurfaced. The civil war ended up costing two million Nigerian lives.

Over fifty years past independence, though some progress has been made to deal with this social ill, Nigerians still identify strongly with their tribes, and vote along tribal lines. They assume that their destiny is linked to their ethnic and religious identity, in other words, their tribe. This means conflicts and politics are usually linked to religion or ethnicity. This makes it hard to fight corruption, since tradition forbids citizens from exposing or prosecuting fellow tribesmen for corrupt practices. Fair employment is challenging because of an unwritten rule that contracts should be awarded to members of the same tribe, which means merit is sacrificed to tribalism, and abuses of power are often overlooked.

Political power tends to overlook intertribal consensus, which means political power just rotates from one party to another. One of the biggest problems caused by this tribalism is distrust. Each tribe distrusts the others, which means legitimate issues, such as poverty and environmental pollution in the Niger Delta for example, are often dismissed as trivial issues when they don't impact the tribe in power.

The 2014 National Conference, which included 492 delegates that represented a cross section of Nigerians, did make an effort to discuss and resolve the country's issues through diversity. It emphasized the need for Nigerians to put aside tribal differences and work together as one harmonious Nigeria.

In my opinion, this isn't just the responsibility of the government; all Nigerians have a role to play in this advancement, including educators and businessmen. We need to work from a place that puts the focus on an individual, not their tribe. To get away from the problems of tribalism, I believe we need to embrace the beauty of our diversity, as Marco Bizzarri averred. Not only should the government be transparent and accountable, all of us need to be so.

Embracing All Cultures

As an Igbo in Uyo, I was an outsider, but I was determined to get past this. I knew that to be included, I needed to be inclusive. I needed to be open and accept people from all of Nigeria's cultures and religions. I knew despite the civil war and despite our tribal differences, there was strength in Nigeria's diversity. People from different tribes had different strengths, and all these strengths combined could solve problems that none of us could solve alone.

Although the notion of inclusion didn't come to fruition in my business until I was rebuilding in Uyo, it had been fermenting in my mind since childhood when I left my village to live in the city with my aunt and came across diverse cultures. It came to mind again when I moved to Eket. Those early travels shaped how I saw people. Many people not of the Igbo tribe helped me, which showed me that we need people, regardless of their tribe or origin. From traveling with the Irish priest, I learned to cut across religion and ethnicity and value everyone equally. Travel made me accepting of people. I knew that every tribe could contribute something to making Nigeria great. My travels also showed me that the best people to do business with are not always the people from your nuclear family, friends, or ethnic group. From my childhood travels, therefore, I learned to openly embrace new people and give them my word.

To harness the power of our diversity as a businessman, I needed to approach business with openness and fairness and deal with everyone faithfully. I was determined to do business in the different cultures and ethnicities across Nigeria appreciating the truism of the Marco Bizzarri statement that "diversity and inclusion, which are the real grounds for creativity, must remain at the center of what we do." I wanted to be a Nigerian doing business in Nigeria. This is why I adopted the core values of inclusion, transparency, and accountability in my company.

Inclusion was key to me because when I got to Uyo, the faces of my clients were not people from my ethnicity. This meant they would doubt me, ask questions, and argue. People from my tribe were often seen as people who wanted fast money, but living in a country with diverse cultures and ethnicities, it was important that people outside my ethnicity didn't see me as perpetuating such stereotypes. If I were to do business successfully in Uyo, I needed them to trust me. It would have been impossible to convince them by myself because they had an answer for every argument I presented. They needed to see my team as if they were family.

Thankfully, one of my team members, Ifiok Umana, who still works with me even after reaching retirement age, was one of the first people who really believed in what I was doing. I met Ifiok Umana when I was trying to talk to people in government and convince them to participate in business with me. He was the desk officer appointed to overseeing the meetings and assessing the situation. He championed my proposal because he believed me.

Working with a person from another tribe was courageous of him at a time when there were still elements of mutual suspicion among different groups. People were skeptical of him for working with me, but over time that changed because of our shared values. I can't express how much his courage meant to me and how it bolstered my vision of a diversified workforce.

In addition, he explained my ideas to those in government meetings and because he believed in me, others trusted him and believed in me despite me being an outsider. Doing business there would have been very different otherwise.

Ifiok believed in me because I was able to show transparency in my dealings with him, and I came to those meetings with some people from his tribe in my team. Some of them were in his church, so he said, "If these people who I know are working with him, I think it's something worth encouraging." This was one of the reasons why he encouraged me.

The Value of Inclusion and Tolerance

In employing a diverse team, I wasn't giving priority to one group over another. I employed people and gave priority to work. I gave priority to what people brought to the table regardless of their tribe or religion. People from the southwest are quick; they want to make money and do well, but they need to understand rules and boundaries. People from the south tend to be loyal and patient. They want to live a good life. People from my tribe are not workaholics. When the workload gets heavy, they may not stick around too long.

Bringing all these people together was challenging. It was important that there wasn't friction between them. It was important to strike a balance between our work ethics so that we could have something powerful. It was important that each person be open to accept the others and the qualities they could bring to the table. At the end of the day, we all had to work together to achieve the same vision for the organization. We all had to adopt a professional and consistent attitude and appearance, which was key in my workplace culture. Each employee had to be transparent and inclusive and tolerant and each had to serve the need of the people first, not the need to hard sell just to close a deal. It was important to me that all my employees pull together as a team around these core values regardless of their ethnic origin.

This diversity ended up bolstering our corporate image. Many people in Nigeria have trouble dealing with people from other tribes, but people looked at our company and saw we were tolerant when it came to religion and culture. Then, because people of all tribes could see they would be accepted, they were willing to work with us.

Outside our company, our message of tolerance helped us be more acceptable to customers. Clients noticed our openness and were accepting of us as a young business. They listened to us. They read our body language. They knew we genuinely cared about them. Many of our competitors still believed and operated from the assumption that "it has to be me and my people." I believed that was myopic. It limited what they could do and prevented them from developing a truly diverse team, which has its attendant advantages.

I wanted to be accepted in Nigeria and have the offices in all the cities I'd listed on my business card when I was sleeping in Sunday's shop in Eket years before. To do this, I knew that I needed to be accepting of everyone from all over Nigeria and beyond. This value stood to us as we grew, because new customers would often ask, "People from my part of the world—are we represented in your company?" When the answer is yes, and when they saw Christians, Muslims, and Buddhists working with us along with representatives from all of the major Nigerian tribes, it created a level of confidence that we were fair and nondiscriminatory. It was clear that the moment someone came to work with me, they wore the badge that said, "It doesn't matter where you're from."

Today, having expanded from one to thirty offices across the country, I still make sure the senior officers know that even though they are not from my tribe, they have a say. They can take positions of importance. They can rise to the highest office. From the customer's perspective, each time we open a new office in the area of a specific tribe, it's still staffed with a cross section of Nigerians from the major tribes.

When I went to talk to people about businesses in different locations or different government offices as we tried to push into the bigger Nigerian market, each of our teams had a balance of people from all the ethnicities: the Hausa, the Yoruba, the Igbo. My team is never made up of people from one ethnic group.

Having an ethnically diverse team yielded better results. Customers listened to us. Not only did the team relate better, it showed people that I didn't take their trust for granted. They asked questions and we answered them. In the end, they were convinced and signed up.

This took a lot of time and effort to achieve this level of diversity, but it was worth it.

The Value of Fairness

Related to cultural diversity is fairness and emphasizing inclusion and tolerance, which leads naturally to my next core value of fairness.

DIVERSITY HELPED US BECOME MORE COURAGEOUS AND MORE PRINCIPLED IN MAKING DECISIONS.

Culturally, diversity helped us become more courageous and more principled in making decisions. We could look critically at things and not be swayed by ethnic or religious prejudice. In some businesses, family and friends receive favorable treatment. For example, if promotions in my company were made by taking into consideration ethnic affiliations, it would hurt others. They might not express their feelings, and might not discuss it in the open, but resentment would fester.

When this happens, other employees are alienated and this limits what you can accomplish. It doesn't encourage employees to be their best, but when they know that you are fair and accepting, they become more loyal and more committed to the company. Therefore, I adopted the core value of fairness in my company. People were rewarded on merit, not on "oh, he's from my tribe; oh, he's my brother; oh, she's my sister." I found many times in my experience that, to manifest a vision, you need people who are competent, not people who are from "my tribe." Oftentimes the people who bring you down are people from your own locality who were employed out of loyalty not for merit.

The Value of Serving the Need

As I focused on serving the need in Nigeria, I changed the Indians' perception of doing business with a Nigerian. They saw me as having a purpose and an agenda that other motorcycle dealers didn't have. This opened the door to more opportunities and gave me the potential to scale up and expand into supplying other products. Eventually, I was able to expand into providing housing, which I'll talk about more in the next chapter.

A big issue in Nigeria was the almost complete absence of a middle class. People were either "up there" or "down here." There was very little in between. For the poor or those trying to squeeze into the middle, life was very hard. I saw in their faces that familiar look of a family struggling. There was a great need there.

Having worked in a bank, I knew how difficult it was for them to get a loan. The banks had been in turmoil—closing or consolidating—and were now looking for more quality customers to bring in more money. This meant there was a class of client that wasn't in the banks' books. These people weren't lucrative, so they were a low priority. There was no real care for the people on the bottom. Even low-earning clients weren't able to get a loan. The poor and middle class needed help with the basics of life and the occasional comfort. This was when I realized that my model didn't need to be limited to motorcycles. I needed to expand my business model to accommodate other needs. I stepped back and asked, "What does the average person really want? What do they lack in their house?"

I realized that many people didn't need the banks at all. Their income was so low, they didn't even need to have accounts with the banks. In many places, the accountant in the government office went to the bank, withdrew the payroll, came back to the office, and paid the workers in cash. I noticed that every month before their payroll came in, they had already spent their salary. They couldn't make ends meet from one paycheck to the next and didn't have always the discipline or know-how to manage their small wages as best they could. This meant it was impossible to get the basic necessities in life, never mind get some comforts like a television.

However, when people heard how they could acquire a motorcycle, I often heard them say, "I wish it was a freezer," or "I wish it was a generator set," or "I wish I could get a laptop for my daughter in school," or "I wish I could get a gas burner." So I picked up all their wishes, then went to work to make them happen.

I started talking to employees directly to identify the many other products they needed. I made a list and figured out how to meet these needs. They needed kitchen equipment, kitchen appliances, refrigeration, and other electrical appliances, including televisions, so we expanded into these items. We started offering ordinary things that they found difficult to acquire. I began to include computers, kitchen appliances, and other products.

I went to the administrator of the corporation or government office with a list of products I knew their employees needed but couldn't acquire and then applied my original business model to these items—having the employer make the down payment and deduct the installments from their salaries each week—in order to supplying these goods. I expanded my supply chain and structured deals with new suppliers the way I had with the Indians in Lagos to acquire these products and have them for resale.

In this way, I replicated my motorcycle model with new products, customers, and suppliers. I took the money that the people contributed to the supplier and got credit extended on that basis. I then used the credit to acquire and supply the products.

This had never been done in Nigeria. It started then as a result of a need in me to get on my feet and to come up with a vision to sustain me into the future. Today, we are one of the biggest companies in Nigeria.

The Value of Adding Value

I have always asked, "How do I add value to your life? How do I make it better?" Each time I do that, I create wealth for myself and for the people around me. On that basis, I have gone from that tiny shop with four employees to over three hundred employees in different cities across Nigeria.

As Amaecom expanded, I didn't follow popular opinion or the established methods of doing business. I didn't do what other people were doing. I was looking for innovative ways to fill the need that was there. I don't just say, "Let's go there; there's so much money there." I was careful to understand the need I was trying to meet and the societal imbalance I was trying to redress. I thought in terms of how could I add to people's lives. I needed to help them acquire these things over time without worrying about them defaulting. That was why the employer-based installment plan worked so well. This made business profitable for me too, so in creating value for them, I created value for myself, and was able to offer employment to a team of people in the process.

An advantage to this business model was that if I could get it right with one set, or one community, or one group, they told other groups. They spread the news initially. I didn't have to advertise. Our customers become our marketers, and that was how we scaled up.

Authentically meeting the need allowed my business to flourish when times were tough and people were going out of business. No matter the climate, I still thought in terms of how could I add true value to the lives of people.

I didn't take a lot of money out of the business to pay myself in those days. I exercised restraint in my own personal extravagances. I was careful about what I spent on the products and drove a modest, but professional car. I got to the point of seeing that if I was going to solve the problem of supplying basic necessities to low income earners, that the money I needed for myself would come and eventually, it did.

A lot of young people came to me saying, "We need money." I tell them, "Look, it's not about money. It's about the idea you have, the problems you want to solve. There is friction everywhere; fit it and you will be successful. Don't be a copycat."

When many people are starting in business, they jump into a business because others are doing it. I tell them, "Look, you don't go into business because a lot of people are going there because this guy looks smart, he looks good, he drives two cars. You think when you go there, you're going to make some money. No, it doesn't work that way." That attitude is sure to land you in some muddy waters. I had to wade in those waters many times. To be successful takes ingenuity and growth, both professionally and personally, as well as a drive to be authentic, serve the need, and add value to other people's lives. In the end, this comes back tenfold.

ON REFLECTION

As I matured as a businessman, I understood the need for our branding to represent what the company stood for and reflect our core values of quality, integrity and passion, which were imbued in our organizational culture, processes, and transactions, resulting to boosted customer confidence. Having a diverse team enabled us navigate cultural issues properly, which in turn boosted our corporate image.

Over time, I understood the importance of having a deeper desire to add value, because it's only when we add value that we can create wealth for ourselves and others. When you have the desire to add value, help will always come, just ask if you share good ideas they will eventually manifest.

Over time, my business model made life easier for everyone. It was a large undertaking, but we managed to juggle all the demands on the supply chain and managing the finance to make it a success. Everyone was happy. Over time, people got excited about the opportunities to have their salary structured in a way that allowed them buy a motorcycles and other products. As word of mouth spread, more people came, and we ended up with a four-star-rated business.

Some of the problems I wanted to help solve were unemployment, public health care, and education. This eventually led to the establishment of a foundation that offered medical care in a small hospital and paid for a few young people into third-level education. Empowering the youth was important to me, not by giving handouts, but by lending them money to start this business of their dreams. However, before I could find ways to support the youth and finance small start-ups, Amaecom needed to undergo further expansion.

CHAPTER 6

Expansion

n the twelve years after I set up Amaecom Global with one small office, two employees, and a vision to have a company with offices all over the world, growth was remarkable. I always had vision and ambition, but even I couldn't have foreseen that we could grow from the little motorcycle shop in Eket, from one tiny office to forty-five offices in three countries, from two to over five hundred employees, and from revenue of 250,000 naira (US $7,000) to 3.5 billion (US $9.7 million).

In those twelve years, I went from busying myself selling motorcycle parts to creating one of the largest asset acquisition companies in Africa, launching our own branded products, a property development venture, and a philanthropic foundation. This success happened because we held fast to our core values and because I never ceased to find a new opportunity to follow on from our last achievement.

Africa Rising

When I started scaling up in Uyo in 2004, Nigerian GDP had reached an all-time high of 19.17 percent and continued at a steady pace averaging 3.9 percent until 2017.[8] Not only was the economy strong, I had the benefit of being part of a wave across Africa called "Africa Rising." The term was coined in the early 2000s to describe the rapid economic growth in sub-Saharan Africa in that decade and the expectation of continued rapid development on the continent. The *Financial Times* described Africa Rising as a "narrative that improved governance [and] meant the continent is almost predestined to enjoy a long period of mid-to-high single-digit economic growth, rising incomes, and an emerging middle class."[9] Since the time when the civil war had left Nigerians with £20 to start over, Nigeria had seen decades of comparative peace, increased consumer spending, and a growing sophistication in information technology. Between 2005 and 2015, the years Amaecom scaled up and expanded, the economy of Africa as a whole increased by 50 percent compared to the global average of 23 percent.[10]

Nigeria emerged as "the Giant of Africa." It is the most populous African country and seventh most populous in the world. Despite being faced with high-profile threats to regional stability, Nigeria is a genuine present-day land of opportunity, with a booming middle class, providing burgeoning asset financing demand and a queue of international companies looking to invest. The population is young; over 70 percent of Nigerians are under thirty. However, 60 percent of

---

8   Average GDP between 1982 and 2017 was 3.9 percent.

9   Steve Johnson, "Africa's Life Expectancy Jumps Dramatically," *Financial Times*, April 26, 2016, https://www.ft.com/content/38c2ad3e-0874-11e6-b6d3-746f8e9cdd33.

10   Peter Fabricius, "Africa Rising or Africa Uprising?" The M&G Online, November 11, 2015, https://mg.co.za/article/2015-11-11-africa-rising-or-africa-uprising.

Nigerian citizens are still living in poverty, due to unequal economic growth and job opportunities. Unable to qualify for loans, more and more people needed alternative sources of finance. This meant Nigeria was primed for the BuyNow PayLater™ model we offered at Amaecom.

I saw Africa Rising as more than just an economic climate. I saw in it a unifying theme drawn from the deeply rooted African values of ambition, openness, hope, and respect. I saw creativity, drive, and imagination, which are vital to Africa's economic future.

Applying these values to our growth and expansion in this land of opportunity meant we never tried to extort profits; we held fast to our vales of quality, integrity, and passion, and played to the strength we had from our cultural diversity and from the scalability advantages inherent in our business model. We increased employment opportunities, met people's needs, and developed an ethical and transparent corporate culture that rewarded us with exponential growth.

Identifying Growth Opportunities

After our initial branching out and scaling up with new products in 2006, my two staff members were still going door to door to clients with a long list of what products were available. It occurred to me that we could reach more people faster if we were to showcase our products in one of the offices and bring the payroll department and all the employees together to see them and learn about our model of BuyNow PayLater™. If we could showcase our products to clients in a central location, we would be able to greatly expand our reach and do it more quickly.

No one had done this before, but I arranged a meeting with a former colleague who worked at the bank and showed him all the individual contracts I'd secured. I said, "Look, all these people have signed up for the different contracts and this is what they want, and they are authorizing you to pay me over a year or six months." When he saw the demand employees had for essentials that they could buy on our payment plan, he saw the merit of bringing all products and parties together in one place and got behind our initiative.

Local and Statewide Expansion

Our agenda aligned with that of the local government, which also wanted to show its authenticity and transparency. I wanted to be able to help their employees to acquire what they needed but also show them that the people with whom they were doing business were genuine. The head of the local government was able to use its business dealings with us as a tool to say, "Look, we are doing very well for the people. We care about their welfare. We've been able to partner with this company." Because we had good banking relationships and a good reputation, local government officials gave us permission to go ahead with the event and parleyed it into a publicity tool by inviting a news crew in to televise it.

Having a news crew interested might sound unusual, but it was an unusual event in Nigeria at the time. The TV crew wanted to know if what we were doing was as good as it sounded. This kind of business model was new. Until then, if a Nigerian needed something, he had to go to the bank, or he'd have to ask for a loan from his employer, which was frowned upon. It was not professional. However, structuring a standard financing model was something the employee could engage in without shame. Another novel aspect of our event was that people often came along promising a deal to sell products to clients, but these business people were rarely honest or transparent. This meant employees were skeptical. To have a company come along with a track record that was vetted by the government was a new concept and was therefore of interest to the news crew.

Thus, one morning in 2006, a convoy of trucks arrived at the local government office at the secondary school board in Akwa Ibom State. We offloaded and assembled the products in an open office and invited the employees to come and see them and talk to us about finance plans. We brought them and the employees together, which helped to enhance our core value of transparency.

Our top clients came in and started the introductions. They told the employees what we were doing and encouraged employees to embrace the offer. They explained that buying products on installments was commonplace in the West. We were then able to explain our finance plan easily. One customer asked, "So with 10 percent of my salary, I can actually get all this and pay it over a year or three years?" People who couldn't afford basic necessities in their homes were amazed that this was possible.

Clients could pick the products they needed and then get approval from their employer to have their wages garnished for the installment payments, which allowed them to sign purchase contracts on the spot. They had options to purchase not only motorcycles, but refrigerators, computers, cooking appliances, and other household products.

Overall, it was a good day. We rented canopies, offered drinks and snacks, and played music. People could sit around and talk and ask questions. The TV crew filmed and aired the event, which meant people all over the province realized they could avail themselves of this opportunity to get what they needed. Demand grew quickly and our cash flow increased dramatically. Each month employers deducted the amount the employee owed for the product they bought and deposited it directly into our bank account. Our balance grew, which meant our collateral grew and new opportunities for growth were presented.

This one event launched Amaecom into a new era. It became apparent that the model of BuyNow PayLater™ that we implemented in Uyo could be expanded to offices across the province and Nigeria at large.

The State Education Board in Uyo local government is one of thirty-one across the state, so after that showcase that day, other local governments wanted to get involved. This meant a lot of meetings for me, as I had to visit each local government. Initially, I was doing these meetings alone, but I soon had to employ and train two more people to help me. In short order, our customer base doubled.

> WE HAD BEEN BUILDING A GOOD REPUTATION FROM OUR EARLIEST DAYS, AND THIS EVENT WAS A BIG ADVERTISEMENT NOT ONLY FOR OUR FINANCING PLAN AND OUR PRODUCTS, BUT ALSO FOR OUR VALUES.

Competitors were asking, "How did you make that happen?" It happened because we had already begun to get into the consciousness of the people. We had been building a good reputation from our earliest days, and this event was a big advertisement not only for our financing plan and our products, but also for our values.

The day was eye-opening for me for another reason. I knew people needed basic necessities, but now I realized they wanted more than that. They wanted to live a good life, and they wanted to have a basic standard of living without having to strive with an inhuman amount of effort to get it. I knew that we could expand on this desire and leverage opportunities as they presented themselves. I needed to start thinking of other products and other assets that I could provide them that would enhance their quality of life. Ideas started percolating in my mind, and in the next few years new ventures would soon come to the forefront.

Nationwide Expansion

Nigeria has six geopolitical zones, each with their own state government under the jurisdiction of the federal government, which is based in Abuja. This means, in each zone, there is the federal government, the state government, and local governments. The federal government controls all the federal staff in the country and the state governments are in charge of all the employment of the states. The local governments control the cities.

We had agreements in place with local and state governments, but in a short amount of time, we built up enough credibility and a solid enough reputation that I now wanted to sign a similar agreement with the federal government. In 2012, I wrote to the federal government to bring our model to federal offices and employees.

I knew if we could come to an agreement with the federal government, we would be able to supply federal government offices all over Nigeria. This had huge growth potential for our company. It also meant we could supply people with products from local warehouses, which would bring our place of business into immediate contact with the people. To do this, we only needed an agreement with the central government in Abuja. All federal employees were paid from there, which meant we would be able to interact with federal employees nationwide. By putting an agreement with the federal government in place, we could get contracts from employees all over the country and send them back to one central office in Abuja. It saved a great amount of time and management.

I arranged with the federal government to replicate our model at the federal level. The officials there requested copies of contracts we had signed with federal employees in Abuja, and upon reviewing them decided to facilitate our BuyNow PayLater™ model for federal employees all across the country. Our staff worked around the clock, traveling to different offices and introducing our products and finance plan in order to secure those contracts. It was a lot of work, but it paid off. Soon we were able to open a permanent office in Abuja, the nation's capital and one of the fastest-growing cities in Africa. We had to relocate staff from Uyo to Abuja to handle the orders and contracts for our products and support them as they trained new staff in that location.

Once we moved our head office to Abuja, we opened an additional ten offices, giving us a total of thirty offices in Nigeria, and one each in the neighboring countries of Ghana and Cameroon, which we set up in partnership with a local businessman in each country. These countries were economically and politically similar to Nigeria and their citizens had similar needs; therefore, our BuyNow PayLater™ model was easy to implement.

To manage the workload and volume of business we were conducting across Nigeria, I decided to consciously create a corporate culture that would embody our core values in every office in the nation. This demanded a reorganization of our corporate structure, building a sense of community, continuing our value of inclusiveness and diversification, and continuing to differentiate ourselves from our competition.

Central to our reorganization was the value of respecting all staff across the country, accepting them regardless of tribe or religion, and building a dialogue around how everyone needed to work together in a professional and transparent way that would enhance the image of our company.

Reorganization

We grew so quickly after our showcase day in Uyo that many changes needed to happen internally and quickly.

Within two years, we had to expand our workforce from three to twelve and move to a bigger office. By 2008, our office had gone from one room to ten. We had staff and space upstairs dedicated to customer service, marketing, accounting, and private offices. The first floor was used as a warehouse and for showcasing products. The days of me being the accountant, customer service manager, HR manager, and managing director were over. All of the work that my original two employees and I had covered together up till now had to be delegated. We had to start building out dedicated departments for accounting and marketing, which we didn't have before.

The years I spent wearing all the hats helped me to effectively delegate. Staff members could benefit from my experience and adopt my core values of quality, integrity, and passion. Because I understood the responsibilities of each department, I knew how to align each department into a single vision. I wanted us as a company to become the leading global grassroots one-stop asset financing company in Africa. I wanted to enhance quality of our customers' lives by providing effective asset acquisition solutions.

For this to work, I could no longer do all the sales meetings myself. There were too many of them and they were too spread out. I had to train people to take these meetings and make our presentations. This had a cascade effect. The more people I sent out, the more people heard about us and wanted to meet us.

To maximize efficiency, we replicated the showcase day in other local government offices. The employees would be assembled, and our sales team would meet with them as a group. Sometimes, the crowd was so big, they needed a public address system. The team introduced our products, explained our financing plan, and answered questions. After that, they collected the names of people who wanted products and financing agreements. They would review the contract with them and have them sign it there in the office. Initially, I went with them, but once they were able to do this on their own, it freed me up to focus on growing and organizing the company.

I hadn't studied business organization but came up with an organogram, or an orgchart, that showed the structure and hierarchy of the company. I created a map to lay out who does what and who reports to whom from me, the MD, to the branch managers, team leaders, accounts, and HR. I'd never learned about this in school, but necessity is the mother of invention, as they say.

From there, I had to train my staff, strategize, devise a marketing plan, and reorganize internally. Each week, for example, we sat down and drew a map of which offices we needed to visit and what we had to do there. Each month, we put together a report. These weekly meetings and monthly reports became necessary to stay on track and ahead of situations before problems had a chance to appear.

Coming back to the table consistently like this helped us reorganize, and it fostered staff bonding. It was the first step we took in creating our corporate culture.

Community

Since we were spread out in different offices, it was important to maintain cohesion in the company's ethics and values. To foster a sense of community, we started celebrating everyone's birthday. This was important because a lot of our employees lived too far from their families to get home during the week to celebrate. We got a cake and everyone came together to sing happy birthday. We'd have drinks and a little office party and then everyone took a piece of cake home. It was a small gesture but a meaningful one. It helped our employees to see that they were valued.

I also implemented something I learned while working in the bank. On the first Friday of the month, we asked everyone to come to the office in their native dress. Everyone looked forward to that. It showed our diversity and celebrated the beauty of that diversity. Something amazing came out of that. To this day, it has strengthened our sense of community and commonality. When a staff member is having a challenge, we are there. When someone is bereaved, we commiserate. If someone gets married, we celebrate.

Many people wanted to work with us. People could see how we operated and what we offered. They had to work hard, but the pay was good. It was hard to remember sometimes that only four or five years earlier a competitor who could offer higher wages poached my entire staff. Now everyone wanted to work at Amaecom.

The key to my personnel success was taking care of staff and their needs, making them happy, and creating a culture of community that gave them a sense of belonging. From there, the financials, profitability, and sustainability took care of itself.

Diversity

Once I'd established a well-organized structure and sense of community, our corporate culture took on an even more important significance for me. It became very focused on building an all-inclusive tribal culture within our company, while at the same time making sure everyone spoke a common language and dressed professionally.

As business expanded over the next few years, I realized we needed to break more ground. We needed to reach more people, and this is when my desire for diversity came even more to the front. I had always employed a diverse workforce. I always believed this to be important in looking forward to a new kind of Nigeria. We have so many tribes and tribal loyalty is paramount.

As word of our business model and purchasing opportunities spread state to state, and as people in one state communicated to friends and families in other states, we began to get calls from other state governments inviting us to come and do presentations and implement our model for their employees. As we expanded into different states and interfaced with different tribes, the need for all-inclusiveness became even more important.

I set out to involve people from every tribe in my company with a more conscious effort than ever. I believed diversity would be a strength. If a customer walked into a local office speaking a local dialect, they were met with an employee of the same tribe who spoke the same dialect. No matter who walked into any of our offices, there was someone there who spoke the customer's dialect and could make them feel comfortable. This was not tribalistic. Nigerians are essentially open, but they tend to gravitate toward their own tribe, and I wanted to establish an authenticity in terms of genuine all-inclusive intention.

Each member on our team brought different strengths to the table. Additionally, when customers saw the diversity in our organization it gave them confidence, it assured them of inclusion, and that built trust. Every team meeting was multi-ethnic. A multi-ethnic team, for example, led a meeting in an Ibo area, but an Ibo team member spoke to potential customers in their own native dialect. The team was always diverse, but there was always someone who could speak the language.

Ethnically diversifying was a little challenging. Not every office had local people from each tribe that I could hire, so I had to hire people who were willing to relocate and arranged accommodation as part of their remuneration package. It took some effort and commitment, but it was worth it. This aspect of our organization set us apart from our competitors.

Inclusiveness

Within a decade of Amaecom's inception, we were spread across three countries and we had to make a concerted effort to maintain cohesion in our corporate culture. Sending emails and telling them of our vision was not good enough. I wanted to bring them all together to allow them experience our cohesion. To accomplish this, I began to organize a one-week conference, or corporate retreat, in Uyo each year for all our staff members. The conference gave us the opportunity to come together for training, but we also made time for fun.

This week of living together in the same hotel, sleeping together, eating together became very important. Some people would get up and go jogging together in the morning. Others would take walks together. These activities created common ground and enhanced our bond. It brought all employees into alignment with a common vision.

The last night of each conference week, we have a party where we can dress in traditional garb and have little competitions. It is a night filled with merriment and laughter. This tradition has become unifying and special.

The retreat allows us perpetuate our ethics and standards and also makes sure our training across offices was consistent in terms of customer care, management, finance, and marketing. We had and continue to have town halls where people can ask questions and talk about what they're doing in their locations. This gives people an opportunity to share their pride in their local offices and community. It proved to be a way to showcase all our offices, but also to inspire each other. When one office heard a colleague tell a story about another location, they were encouraged to explore those options themselves and even come up with their own innovative ideas.

I learned from my years leading these meetings that when you're able to sit with employees and listen to them and talk about their challenges, you offer an opportunity for everyone to speak. In meetings, people couldn't just come and sit down. They had to talk, they had to interact with me. I got to know every employee by their first name, and that gave them a sense of inclusion. Then when I go back to the head office in Abuja, I tell them that they can still reach out to me. This is important. When you're able to give them that support, you are saying, "You are valued, and it does matter where you come from." This is an HR job, but I started this approach to make sure that people are happy and comfortable. That motivates people to strive to meet their goals and give back to the company.

In the course of any workday, staff members and I eat together. I greet them with a hug. This in turn inspires the local office managers to do the same. In Nigeria, I didn't come across other companies doing this. I do know a bank that values employees, but it doesn't interact with them in this way.

FROM MY CHILDHOOD LIVING WITH MY AUNT AND MIXING AND MEETING PEOPLE FROM DIFFERENT TRIBES AND DIFFERENT WALKS OF LIFE, THE IDEA OF WELCOMING AND VALUING ALL KINDS OF PEOPLE BECAME IMPORTANT TO ME.

Nobody told me how to develop a bond across the company between employees, or even that it was needed. It was an intuitive decision on my part. I always believed there was a need for Nigerians to come together. From my childhood living with my aunt and mixing and meeting people from different tribes and different walks of life, the idea of welcoming and valuing all kinds of people became important to me. It was a great early learning experience. It has benefited me greatly in terms of staff loyalty and profitability. Employees are more invested in the company, and they are always looking for ways to do better.

Everyone has taken our values to heart of quality, integrity, and passion. They reflect these values back to our customers. When you hire people from different backgrounds, especially people who are not professionals, it's important to groom them. Initially, some employees were interested in making more money for the company, rather than satisfying the customer. They thought, "Oh, if I could just make more money, I'll get promoted, I'll be loved by my company, I'll be loved by my boss." Of course, the employees do have a goal to be able to achieve certain numbers and meet particular targets, but beyond that I try to show them that it is the quality of our service and the transparency in our dealings that is key to us going far as a company. Over time, they learned that our way is being passionate about our customers' happiness.

Business needs to be about more than making profits; it needs to be sustainable in the long term. How do you sustain the company for the next ten years? The answer comes down to whether you want to remain in business in the next ten years or whether you only want to make a profit and go home. At Amaecom, we focus on the former, and this influences how we attend to our customers. We put ourselves in our customers' shoes. This attitude however isn't something that staff members can learn behind a desk. They need to see it from the boss. It needs to trickle down, and this trickle down starts with how the staff are treated. If you want employees to treat customers well, then your employees have to be treated well too.

I think of my employees as my first customers. If I am able to treat them well in honesty and transparency, they will treat the customer in the same way.

The Passion to Differentiate

In the years following the televised coverage of our event, our company grew 500 percent. We devised a better financial plan to allow our clients meet their obligations. Payments were deposited into the Amaecom account, which made the bank more amenable to offering us loans to expand. I still had to provide collateral if I wanted a loan, but having cash already deposited there made obtaining a loan much easier.

The company was expanding so quickly, I needed to increase our working capital to buy appliances, generators, motorcycles, etc. in much greater quantities to meet the demand for BuyNow PayLater™ contracts. I also needed to able to meet the needs of the customer in new ways, which meant figuring out intuitively what I needed to do to keep the company growing.

For my first loan, I used my three-room house in Eket as collateral. My wife and children still lived there. When I went home to get the deeds of the house to give to the bank as collateral, my wife wasn't happy.

"Do you want to sell the house again?" she asked. "You've just gotten out of trouble, and now you're offering the deeds up again as collateral to the bank. What happens in a month from now?"

I assured her I had a long-term plan, and I did. From the start of my career, I knew I wanted to build an organization that would last. I wanted to leave a legacy. I wasn't anxious about making fast money or short-term profits, which was the focus of many of my competitors. I always looked to surviving in the long term by doing something different. I wanted to keep moving forward. I never wanted to go back to where I'd been, so I wanted my own branded products. With that in mind, I traveled to China to the company where I had developed a relationship during my motorcycle business. Hence when the opportunity to explore the Chinese manufacturing company came through a trade fair, I maximized that opportunity in 2009, and it turned out to be a productive visit where I made some good contacts. One of the contacts I met there was Lisa Qiu. She attended most of the trade shows because she was a sales rep for one of the big importers and manufacturers of goods from China. She was highly intelligent, keen to learn, and very honest. I explained exactly what we wanted to do, and she helped me identify good manufacturers.

I took meetings with those whom she recommended and decided to enter into an agreement with one of them to make water dispensers for our market in Nigeria. This was followed later by freezers and generators—the two products in highest demand in Nigeria.

One of my conditions for the manufacturer was that every product we were going to buy and sell under our brand name had to meet UK or US standards. I insisted that even though the products were going to Nigeria, each product had to have a AAA rating. Before we engaged a manufacturer, that had to be understood and guaranteed.

The reason for my inflexibility on this issue came from what was called at some point the "Nigerian standard." People from Nigeria going to Chinese factories were asked where they were from or in which market they would be selling. When a manufacturer learned it was Nigeria, the business owner would be sold a different quality product. In other words, factories were selling lower quality products to wholesalers in third-world countries than they were selling to the US. This was likely because low quality products were also low cost and that was all third-world residents could afford.

Unfortunately, all too often companies are more focused on the bottom line and not the welfare of people. Factories made products that would break soon after the sale, but no one cared other than the end user. Wholesalers were living the good life. They sold in bulk quantities and customers never saw the inside of those warehouses. The manufacturers never got consumer feedback and probably didn't care. However, because we were involved from manufacturing to the end product for the user, we would be interfacing all along the line from production to final sale. This meant we had to make sure when we saw those customers face to face, that they were satisfied. In addition, our customers were paying over the course of one to two years. We needed to make sure the quality of the product lasted longer than their repayment period. We didn't want people buying appliances that were broken before they'd even finished paying them off.

This long-term, legacy-based vision set us apart from our competitors. However, to remain dominant in the market, we had to offer products that were of a quality we could guarantee. This of course made our products more expensive. Ordinarily, these prices would be beyond the reach of our customer, but our BuyNow PayLater™ finance structure meant they could afford to buy these higher-quality products. They were willing to pay the additional cost because they knew they were getting quality that would last.

For example, generators use a coil. Some manufacturers use aluminum or a mix of aluminum and copper. The best quality is copper, good copper, but wholesalers would tell the Chinese factories to use 50 percent copper and 50 percent aluminum. Once that happens, the cost of production is lowered and the cost to the end user is lowered, but the quality of the generator is greatly diminished. We insisted that our coils be 100 percent copper. I didn't want to be bringing generators to the market that would only last two years and be broken before the customer had even paid off the outstanding purchase price. It was important to work hard to show that we were giving them authentic products. Not only that, we prioritized the comfort of clients in the production of products. For example, our generators were designed with remote control ignitions so that our clients could start their generators from the comfort of their rooms while our competitors used keys and manual effort. This was a game changer for our business, and our staff in China was also proud of the products they were making for us. They could see how we were doing things differently.

Soon, the Chinese manufacturers recognized that we were different, as did the end users in Nigeria. Seeing a Nigerian company bring products of this quality into the Nigerian market under a domestic company brand name was unique. When people bought our products, they knew they were buying something reliable that was worth the extra cost. People knew that if I put our brand name on a product, I knew what I was doing. This also paved the way for our sales team to close new contracts. From that point on, when we went to new locations and new states and presented our business model, we were going in with our own product with our own brand. We could give sample products to government offices so they could see the quality of what we offered.

Having our own product line also increased our credibility. People had the perception that if we had our own product line, we must be a big company, not a start-up that would disappear within a year. This also gave us an edge on our competition, as I predicted, because they couldn't offer their own branded products, and we offered ours exclusively through Amaecom to our customers.

Cutting out the wholesaler also gave us more control over our pricing. Obviously, some products we couldn't brand, such as computers, so the computers our customers bought from us they could get anywhere, but we could determine the price for our water dispensers, generators, and freezers, which they could only get from us.

A year later, the company Lisa Qiu had been working for went bankrupt, so I employed her at Amaecom to work for us in China. It worked out well, because she could dedicate her time to our needs and make sure we were getting products that aligned with our quality standards. Today, when we start working with a new manufacturer, she visits the factory and has discussions. If she recommends them, I fly there for meetings and negotiate the level of quality demanded and the terms of our agreement.

We later opened a factory in Nigeria to manufacture mattresses because it was one of the products people demanded. Many customers had been sleeping on the same mattress for twenty or thirty years. This was one problem Nigerian families had that I could solve. I acquired some land in Uyo and opened a factory to employ Nigerians to manufacture mattresses. Our technology products, such as refrigerators, freezers, generators, and water dispensers, needed to be produced in Chinese factories because of the level of skill required, but I didn't need to go to China to manufacture mattresses. I could find people with the skill set in Nigeria to make them. This meant we were able to offer domestic employment opportunities and sell the mattresses on the same BuyNow PayLater™ model. Again, my motive was not to start this line for its great profit potential but to help meet the needs of the people. I dreamt about touching lives, having a good life for myself and others. This idea was inspired by my early years in the city far from my village where I saw different tribes and genders all striving for excellence and inclusion and welcoming what people of all backgrounds had to offer. At the end of the day, the venture was profitable because of this.

After the launch at the government office that day, people came to me with different ideas for what they wanted to acquire. So we started to ask that question: What else do you need to acquire? People came back with a long list, so we took that list and started to consciously plan ways to help them.

Passion for Young Entrepreneurship

It wasn't only individual citizens who were struggling to finance their asset needs. Many people in the Uyo area weren't able to start a business despite having good ideas. I wanted to help entrepreneurs get a start. For example, one person wanted to set up a business center where people could go in and use computers, whether they wanted to send emails, print, bind documents, or take care of basic office-related stationery needs. They couldn't get a loan to acquire generators or computers or even coffee machines. This was an area where we could grow. We supplied the business equipment for them on a BuyNow PayLater™ scheme. Another person wanted to set up a restaurant and another a small theater that needed good sound equipment. Our ability to help young entrepreneurs start up small businesses eventually evolved into a mentorship program for young up-and-coming business students, which I'll talk about more in Chapter 9.

Learning and Networking

To guarantee survival and sustainability, businesses must evolve and be adaptable. This is achieved through continuous learning. Not only does continuous learning help workforce/talent development, it enhances orga-

> **TO GUARANTEE SURVIVAL AND SUSTAINABILITY, BUSINESSES MUST EVOLVE AND BE ADAPTABLE.**

nizational competitiveness, agility, and engagement. To this end, I began to promote personal development through continuous professional development in my company.

My quest for personal development led me to the Entrepreneurs' Organization (EO) in 2014, and the Asia Bridge Forum in 2017, where I took moderators training in conjunction with people from the Middle East, Pakistan, and Cape Town in South Africa. I also attended the Commonwealth Head of Government meeting in Malta, and the One Level Summit in Munich. Joining EO gave me the opportunity to hone my leadership skills because I knew that as my business grew, my management skill had to grow, too. In one of its training sessions on team building, I realized that the role of the leader is akin to the conductor of an orchestra whose task is to see that the various units, ranging from brass to woodwind, strings and percussion, are playing in sync. Done right, a beautiful performance results, but should the conductor perform poorly, so does the orchestra. This applies to business. Another useful takeaway from one of its training sessions was the need for transformation and growth in business using the life cycle of a butterfly: innovation prompts the metamorphosis of an organization from one level to another.

Similarly, joining the Asia Bridge Forum provided me with the opportunity to meet other inspired entrepreneurs to discuss issues and challenges facing business. We once had a discussion about regulations that impede business growth and the ease of doing business, and came up with better ways to resolve and navigate these challenges. We also discussed important trends for the future of businesses.

In terms of personal development, I had the chance to meet brilliant minds at the Massachusetts Institute of Technology, where I made some lifelong friendships. Joining these organizations also offered networking opportunities, which had a positive influence on me as an individual and on my company. It connected me with peers who offered candid advice on business matters, business opportunities, and important referrals.

These insights also allowed me to invest in my staff and improve their motivation, efficiency, and effectiveness on the job. In this way, we became a learning organization.

ON REFLECTION

Once we secured our place in the market by focusing on acting according to our passion to make life better for people and offering quality products that aligned with our integrity, I hired a TV production company to create a commercial, just a simple two-minute commercial, made with a local comedian called Ime Bishop. He is now famous, but back then he was unknown. He got into one of our freezers and then opened the door and jumped out, saying, "Amaecom, I better pass my neighbor oh," which is Pidgin English for "I'm better than my neighbor." The ad ran for three years and that slogan spread all over Nigeria. Eventually, the Nigerian Broadcasting Corporation took it off the air for fear kids would copy Ime Bishop and climb into the freezers themselves. However, our message to customers continued. It said, "If you sign on to do business with us, your life is going to get better because you don't need more money to get what you want; you can live comfortably now."

After twelve years of hard work, my focus on quality, integrity, passion, and meeting the needs of others eventually allowed me to meet the needs of my own family. I relocated with Chika and my children to Abuja, which was a promise I had made her five years earlier when there wasn't even a hint of us having a reach that extended anywhere near that city, never mind a head office there.

*Marcel always knew where he was going. He told me after
we had built a house in Eket, and we were doing okay, that
we were going to live in Abuja within the next five years.
He always said things that eventually came to pass.*

CHIKA OFOMATA

My first five-year plan had been fulfilled. Now it was time for a
new five-year plan that would allow me to continue to build on my
core values, not only to be the premier asset financing company in
Nigeria, but also to leave a legacy based on that drive, which led me
into meeting the next great need with the most ambitious plan ever:
to tackle the housing crisis in Nigeria.

CHAPTER 7

A Venture into Property Development

The real estate business is not something I ever thought I would get into, but just like every other business I started, it came about by focusing on the needs of the people.

Nigeria has a pronounced housing deficit. The country has an urbanization rate of 4.39 percent and a housing production of approximately only one hundred thousand units per annum when seven hundred thousand units per annum are needed.[11] This has left the country with a deficit of seventeen million houses and rising.[12] The three main revenue streams for housing production are private developers, foreign direct investment, and the federal and state government budgets. Unfortunately, the government

---

11   "Housing Finance in Nigeria," Centre for Affordable Housing Finance Africa, September 2016, http://housingfinanceafrica.org/countries/nigeria/.

12   Calabar Anietie Akpan, "Nigeria's Housing Deficit Hits 17 Million," *The Guardian*, January 28, 2018, https://guardian.ng/news/nigerias-housing-deficit-hits-17-million/.

budget allocation is grossly inadequate and private developers focus on high-income earners. However, the fastest-growing demographic in Nigeria is the working class.

Part of the challenge with undertaking property development projects in Nigeria—and one of the reasons no one had built a house in ten years for the middle class—has been due to the lack of consistent government housing policy. Nevertheless, our research showed there was a staggering number of people who could afford a reasonable house if the financing were based on a commitment to pay over the duration of their working lives.

The most obvious solution to the problem of providing affordable housing lay in cooperation between the government and private developers by providing tax waivers, density bonuses, reduced land charges, and available financing. That's where Amaecom came in.

Tackling the Housing Crisis

I had been working with people who had jobs in Nigeria, Ghana, and the Cameroon. Many of them weren't able to afford basic appliances until they came into our BuyNow PayLater™ program, but I began to hear more and more that none of them were able to afford a house. The banks didn't offer mortgages to this income class, and even if they did, the cost of acquiring a house and paying back those mortgages was prohibitive. If I wanted to consider Amaecom as a true one-stop shop that supplied the basic necessities of life, we needed to help people to own their own home.

When this problem came to my attention, it coincided with calls coming from different quarters asking if I would consider entering this sector to help alleviate the crisis.

One of the people who asked me to consider doing business in the housing sector was Mrs. Ekerebong Akpan, who is head of the civil service in Akwa Ibom State. I met her when I arrived in Uyo in 2004, when she was a regular civil servant, but over the years she advanced to be head of the civil service training center. She had watched my organization grow from one office to thirty across three countries. She came to me with the suggestion that I look into property development using the BuyNow PayLater™ model to help alleviate the housing crisis.

In 2017, I decided to apply our tried and tested model to housing to bridge the housing market gap. I had some experience with the logistics of actually building. I'd built my own home back in Eket. In the years since then, I was involved in building permanent offices and a few houses here and there across the country. Most of these I built from scratch, so while I didn't have much experience dealing with town planning, permits, and regulations on a scale that large, I did have some knowledge of the building process itself. From there, I set out to find builders and architects who could help me to plan communities with houses, streets, facilities, and shops.

Immediately, I was beset with challenges, restrictive regulations, and technicalities. I knew it would take the same passion, drive, and transparency that gave people hope in our other asset acquisition areas to overcome them. I

> **I WAS DRIVEN BY THE BELIEF THAT IF SOMEONE WORKED FOR THIRTY YEARS, THEY SHOULD BE ABLE TO OWN THEIR OWN HOME TO RETIRE IN.**

was driven by the belief that if someone worked for thirty years, they should be able to own their own home to retire in, which made me determined to make this work.

Feasibility Assessment

Over the years, I'd traveled, networked, and made friends in every sector, with politicians and with businessmen. I had studied at Harvard. I had friends in Chicago who were property developers. I met businessmen on trips to China who were building the components for uniform houses and shipping them to small communities to be built there.

To assess the feasibility of the project, I had access to the employees' payroll, so I knew how much they earned and how much they could afford to pay. The construction costs had to be determined so that the cost of the house was within that range.

After that, I looked at what worked in other countries, asked questions, and came back to have conversations with politicians in Nigeria. I offered workable proposals that were people centric. I knew that if we put the needs of the people first and found a way to build these houses at a cost that they could afford to pay out of their salaries each month that the profit would take care of itself.

I learned a lot when I joined the Nigerian German Business Association and the United States Commercial Service (CS), the trade promotion arm of the US Department of Commerce's International Trade Administration, and the Nigerian Chamber of Commerce Industry and Manufacturing Association (NACCIMA). Between these associations, I had opportunities to meet entrepreneurs from other parts other world, which afforded me much learning and inspiration that I took back to Amaecom.

From there, I set out step by step. Under the Nigerian constitution, all land belongs to government, so I began by writing to different government offices to ask for land to develop a community for people who had paid jobs and wanted to retire into their own homes. Buying land in Uyo is very expensive, so negotiating that deal was the first big challenge. After much negotiation, we reached a preliminary agreement to acquire some land for a premium to be repaid in installments over time. It took three years of applying and waiting.

The arrangement was such that, once the installments were paid, Amaecom would own the land on which we planned to build the houses. It wasn't a massive landmass—not large enough to build a city, but enough to build a housing development that would require a certain amount of town planning, schools, and shops. Since it was my first time in this kind of venture, I thought it best to start relatively small until I learned to navigate the challenges of politics and personal interest in the powers that be. Regulations were intricate, compromises to the design were many, and our effort to keep costs low so that people could afford the houses on the BuyNow PayLater™ model was challenging. Nevertheless, we persevered to find ways around cumbersome, archaic, and sometimes obstructionist policies.

I wanted Amaecom to be a one-stop shop for everything people needed—moveable assets and nonmovable assets. I wanted them to be able to acquire these assets and build the repayment into the salaries they would earn for the rest of their working lives. It was a way I could help improve their lives, and a model that would be profitable enough to allow Amaecom to continue to expand reach people. In this respect, we were different from other property developers whose focus was profit and who were building houses for the upper class customer who could afford to pay outright. However, I knew there was another market in Nigeria—the working-class market. It was just a matter of creating a model and structuring a finance plan to make it feasible.

The acres the government allocated to me were being rented to farmers at the time of the allocation. The government wrote to the farmers and announced our development plans. We then went and talked to the community of farmers and compensated them for their cash crop. Essentially, we were able to make them an offer to cede us the land without hardship. That's how it works in Nigeria. You come to an agreement with the government, and then you have to come to an agreement with the local chief. Once this was all completed, we were ready to put our team in place and get started.

Royal Citadel Value Homes

I set up a new company, Royal Citadel Value Homes. I decided to develop a special kind of team to manifest this vision. We created prototypes of the houses that we could build on the acres of land I acquired from the government. This way we ended up being able to keep costs low to ensure people could afford to pay their monthly payments from their salaries while we were to build part of the house, the structure, the roof, and one or two rooms. After that, the owner could move into the house and finish it under the supervision of our team. Most houses are completed when they go to market, making them too expensive for workers to afford them. This plan would reduce the cost to them and make acquiring a house possible.

Next, the town-planning phase started. I assembled a team of town planners, architects, engineers, structural engineers, and mechanical engineers. We went in and assessed and reassessed the land to optimize our plans. We started surveying, clearing the space, building roads, and mapping out the development.

At this time, the land acquisition, planning, and surveying was being financed out of the Amaecom reserve. I intended to get as far as laying out the town and the developments and building one sample house. Then, once all the relevant agencies signed off, I intended to talk to other investors to partner to finish the four hundred fifty houses in

Uyo, with a view to replicating this model elsewhere. In addition to the sale of the houses on the BuyNow PayLater™ model, a development that size was also attractive to investors interested in building schools, shopping centers, or recreational centers.

It took some work to navigate outmoded government policies and to bring together a team on such a large scale for our new venture into property development to meet the needs of the people. So far, despite the challenges that come from breaking new ground with something unique, our progress has been encouraging. We are well underway in building the first two hundred and twenty houses on our BuyNow PayLater™ scheme. We expect this plan to go as well as all our other ventures that succeeded because they were fundamentally motivated by the needs of humanity and conducted with honesty and transparency, and, like all our other projects, once this one is finished, we have a model to replicate all over Nigeria.

CHAPTER 8

Giving Back

n 2013, I set up the Marcel Ofomata Foundation with my wife, Chika, to contribute in a number of ways to the people of Nigeria as a private organizations focused on advancing the frontiers of humanitarianism, welfare, and philanthropy, especially to the underprivileged.

Before setting up the foundation, finding ways to give back had always been part of my life, but now I am able to put a structure in place to offer scholarships, mentorships, skills training, seed funding for women and youths, and facilitate health-care missions. As Winston Churchill said, "We make a living by what we get. We make a life by what we give."

> "WE MAKE A LIVING BY WHAT WE GET. WE MAKE A LIFE BY WHAT WE GIVE."

We set up the foundations with five objectives:

1. Subsidize education and academic activities through educational scholarship and grants.

2. Bring health-care services to everyone who needs them and encourage scientific-based health care to reduce adult and infant mortality.

3. Develop the capacity of our youths and women through skill acquisition, training, and seminars to make them useful to themselves and society.

4. Encourage, motivate, and mentor those who need role models.

5. Offer microfinancing to those with business ideas that need alternate means of seed capital for start-ups.

The foundation didn't come into existence overnight. For many years, I had been helping with health-care missions, mentoring, and paying the school fees of a number of students. Being able to expand on these efforts has proven to be very rewarding.

For many years, I had been offering informal mentorships in the form of advice to aspiring entrepreneurs about their career path and had been paying school fees for underprivileged students who showed potential and drive. It began with students who found their way to me through various organizations of which I am a member and through my church. These students had known me from the beginning. They knew of my struggles to get established, and they had seen Amaecom go from success to success, so they knew I had learned how to survive and thrive. They would come to me and ask my advice on various ventures. As my company gained prominence, other students began to write to me from universities or invite me to speak at an event in their school. It became a great platform for sharing my experience with them.

While this informal mentoring started off well, the numbers of students seeking advice eventually got too big to manage. I was being asked to speak at many schools and to come and give out awards. My office was filled with letters from people asking for feedback on their ideas. It was clear that a more formal structure was needed. There was a need to have a budget and governance, as well as a balance between social functions and meeting the business needs of my company. That's when I had the idea of setting up a foundation, which would be a wonderful opportunity to give back as a corporate citizen.

Health Care Missions

I didn't know anything about setting up a foundation, but I had been working with an NGO called Imabridge Africa in the US. They came to Nigeria to do a medical mission. As soon as I saw their work, I knew I wanted to extend this mission to my community in Isoufia and the surrounding area.

As the youth president or the youth chairman in my community in Isoufia, I had recognized that we needed a community hospital, a small clinic that could care for the health of the locals. In 2012, with the help of some friends, I built a small institution. A year after that, I met a group of people at Imabridge Africa through Rotary International in Uyo. One of them was Reverend Father Godwin Asuquo from Patrick's Catholic Church in Illinois. He comes from Uyo, but he runs a foundation in Chicago, and each year he and a number of colleagues come here to run a mobile hospital to provide health care to the people of Uyo.

They were doing some very good work, so I approached them

with the idea of extending their services to my state. They agreed. They paid their way to Nigeria and brought medicines from the US, and I paid their accommodations here and footed the medical care bill.

In 2015, we offered our first four-day medical mission in partnership with Imabridge Africa that provided eleven free major/minor medical surgeries, free diagnosis/treatment, free malaria/typhoid treatment, free eye/blood group evaluation, free tests/tablets donation, general body checkup, weight check, medical referral, and free health consultancy, among numerous other services. Today, we recruit doctors from all over Nigeria to help, so that about fifty medical professionals now come to Isuofia to our medical mission. Last year, we had up to three thousand people attend over the three days we were there.

There is a great need for these missions in Nigeria. The government alone can't meet the medical needs of the citizens, so we have taken matters into our own hands to help the sick and provide preventative care, and it has been incredibly successful, and incredibly gratifying to be able to give so much back.

Educational Scholarships

I decided to expand my mentoring work to include offering scholarships to the underprivileged and mentorship programs to those with a keen interest in running sustainable and successful businesses that would give back to society.

I started out by going to smart but underprivileged kids in my hometown of Isuofia and offering to pay their tuition. Three people who worked with me at Amaecom came with me to Anambra State. One was a retired university lecturer and the other an active university lecturer. They arranged a town hall meeting and announced that I would be offering educational scholarships to students. Over the next weeks and months, the two professors gathered information on the candidates and sent me a list of students whose fees needed to be paid.

It worked very well, and students gained an opportunity to study that they would not otherwise have had. Later, I went to the University of Uyo and said, "I want to help students who are struggling, who maybe can't afford their fees but who are talented. I'm going to offer them a grant and pay their tuition." We ended up with over fifty students from all over Africa in our scholarship program.

Mentorship Program

While the business students in our scholarship program were doing well, there were other students who also needed help—not necessarily financial help, but they needed guidance. Thus, the foundation's flagship mentorship program was set up to give hope to the underprivileged and encouragement to the talented.

I began to meet with students once a month in Uyo and once a year in Isuofia, where I offer a seminar to answer their questions and give them business advice.

> THE FOUNDATION'S FLAGSHIP MENTORSHIP PROGRAM WAS SET UP TO GIVE HOPE TO THE UNDERPRIVILEGED AND ENCOURAGEMENT TO THE TALENTED.

This proved to be very productive. Students were able to gather and tell their stories, which encouraged other students to be more proactive in their entrepreneurial careers. Many of these students got involved in community development. Last year on my birthday, they hired a hall, threw a birthday party for me, and gave me an award to thank me for inspiring them. It was wonderful.

Today, some of those students are working at Amaecom. Others have their own businesses. One has a small fashion house, another a photography studio, another set up a structural engineering business, and another an architectural practice. They are working hard out on their own, taking care of themselves and their families.

Skills Acquisition

I soon realized the best way forward in terms of helping people acquire the skill and know-how they needed to set up their own businesses was to set up a business school where students could come together, pitch their ideas, devise plans, and get the feedback of experts.

The employment landscape has changed significantly in Nigeria since the end of the civil war. Once, college graduates could get a white-collar job in a bank, but currently it is a challenge, and they don't offer the perks they once did. Because of this, I decided to try to engage with students while they are still in college to mentor them, support them, and help them work out their ideas. This became part of my mentorship program that focused on helping them develop marketable skills.

To be effective in this area, I founded the Mitchell & Michelle Business School (M&M) in 2014 to educate and raise marketplace leaders in the art and science of building and running successful businesses. I wanted to give them sustainable skills and empower them to become independent entrepreneurs in the Nigerian economy today. I wanted to create employment opportunities and help the government in achieving a robust socioeconomic development in order to drive other sectors of the economy.

I recognized there was a knowledge gap in Nigeria. Students weren't getting practical training in schools and colleges, but there was a need to train people with a hands-on approach and then bring them together in an environment where they could interact and exchange ideas. This helped fill the knowledge gap I noticed in the education and training of young entrepreneurs in Nigeria.

The school isn't part of the foundation—it's self-funded—but it shares the aims of the foundation in many ways. I head the school, but the faculty is made up of people who have skills in a variety of trades. We have lawyers, former government workers, and various types of entrepreneurs who have excelled in their respective industries or careers whose collective strength to mentor the M&M students, provide them with practical training, and help them go in the right direction.

Initially, the M&M school had an enterprise club where young people come together in one small office, but today it has grown to twenty offices. When people come in with good ideas, we provide them with an office space, electricity, and internet access so they can sit there and work, like a hub.

Today, some of the program members learned how to sew and set up dress shops. One learned to make juice and now sells juice to banks and ships in the docks. Each has the potential to scale up. I am particularly interested in ideas that are scalable. If a good idea is presented, we look into the possibilities to make this happen for them.

Seed Financing for Women and Youths

I realized that entrepreneurial support wasn't only needed in the cities; there was a need to support women and youths in rural areas too. These two groups are disadvantaged. They are the bedrock of a family, so helping them could help strengthen society.

I came across many women who were trying to set up small businesses in their local areas but hadn't the means to do so. Many of these women were involved in farming, raising pigs and chickens, while others were traders. The traders would go into very rural areas, buy foodstuffs, and bring those to the open market to sell. These were very small enterprises because none of these women had any capital to build their business. I felt it was important to give them a chance to grow, so I started with the women in my own community.

I started out by asking one woman with status in the community to gather the other women in the town for a meeting to propose my plan to offer microfinancing loans if they wanted to expand. Our arrangement was that they could borrow a small seed capital fund of between fifty thousand and two hundred thousand naira. This is equivalent to only a few hundred dollars but has decent buying power in Nigeria. This loan is repayable without interest within one year. If they have done well and can pay back their loan, they can borrow more money to expand further the next year. In this way, we can monitor their progress and help them while making them accountable. They have to be profitable to pay back their loan and get another, so they have an incentive to succeed. This has been revolving since inception with default of about 1.5 percent.

Engaging the Youth

I believe that everyone should be given fair treatment and opportunities regardless of cultural differences. We believe that society can advance and we can live in a peaceful social order by mentoring, advocating for, and empowering the youth to become successful leaders. This can be done through business leadership, but also through cultural leadership.

Another way of supporting, encouraging, and inspiring youths in Nigeria has been through the Nigerian Peace Corps, which offers a true definition of patriotism through an aggressive campaign for the maintenance of peace, orderliness, respect for constituted authorities, strategic surveillance, and employment.

I decided to get involved and support the Peace Corps, because it helped the unemployed and offered different types of training and different ways of engaging as a responsible citizen. This is particularly important in areas in Nigeria where there is high unemployment. Even if someone is unemployed, that doesn't mean they can or should be lazy, so I lend support to any organization that keeps them engaged. Any society where large numbers of youths are not engaged will become an unsafe society. Poverty and unemployment can give rise to violence and civil disturbance.

> SOCIETY CAN ADVANCE AND WE CAN LIVE IN A PEACEFUL SOCIAL ORDER BY MENTORING, ADVOCATING FOR, AND EMPOWERING THE YOUTH TO BECOME SUCCESSFUL LEADERS.

Nigerian youths, however, are industrious and innovative. They want to be engaged. This is why I'm passionate about the mission of the Peace Corps and why last year I donated an operational vehicle to them to support their effort to engage the youth of Nigeria in responsible citizenship.

For youngsters, I sponsor a traditional Igbo dance troupe. I watched children come home from school on holidays and have nothing to do. I thought it would be good to keep them busy, so I brought in a professional choreographer to teach them to dance and provided grants for them to travel to competitions. Today, they go to different cities to compete and perform. Sometimes they win a little money, but they always get exposure. Today, they have started making money outside the competitions. People hire them to perform at functions, such as marriages or government events. When my friends come from the mission in the US, they always perform for them. The troupe has become a thing of joy for the community, too. The reward that came to me from my work over the years with meeting people's needs in Amaecom and facilitating their future in the foundation, was the recognition by my kinsmen. In 2016, I was conferred with the honorary chieftaincy title of Onwa Isuofia. The event attracted many people who came out to honor me for my positive impact on humanity. His Royal Highness, Igwe Muoghalu of Isoufia, said, "You are an illustrious son; you have done the community proud." It was an unbelievable honor to receive this from my own tribe.

I was later given the chieftaincy title in Benue State (North Central Nigeria) from the Idoma Kingdom as the "Akpa K' Idoma" (meaning the bridge that connects Idoma Kingdom and the outside world) by His Royal Majesty Agabaidu Elias Ikoye Obekpa, and as the "Obong Unwan" by His Royal Majesty Ediden Apostle (Dr.) Ntoeng Udo Effiong Akpan, chairman of the Akwa Ibom State Council of chiefs. This was a huge event. I have been given chieftaincy titles from different tribes in Nigeria, which is a great honor, for the work I have done in diversification. It shows interethnic acceptance and recognition for how I have affected their lives. It shows they appreciate that I'm not ethnically focused or sectional and that I have accepted people from all tribes in my organization. It was humbling for me to have three chieftaincy titles from three major ethnic groups in Nigeria, having received over 103 awards of excellence, honor, and recognition for philanthropic efforts, particularly in the areas of employment creation, economic development, growing of SMEs, and progressive philanthropy for socioeconomic progress, including the International Peace Medal from United Nations. I could not be prouder.

ON REFLECTION

In the last few years, the foundation has brought me great joy. It has given me a great sense of accomplishment. I see its success everywhere I go: in the streets, in the universities, in my village. Everywhere I see reflected back the people whose lives I have touched. Nothing is more powerful than that. It is the greatest joy on earth.

The philanthropy work of the foundation in particular brings people together and inspires young people. It shows them that you can be transparent and honest and still earn a good living and be successful. It shows them that regardless of what some politicians do, the private sector can invest in the country. It shows them that they can and should take pride in their country.

I believe in this country. I believe in the possibilities for my country. I also believe that Nigeria has given me the opportunity and the environment in which I could grow. Why would I not seek to affect the lives of people in a positive way every day?

There will always be naysayers and people who don't understand you. They don't understand that my aim is to add value to the lives of others—not making huge profits and acquiring a lot of possessions at others' expense. The philosophy that guided us to set up the foundation is that "the growth and development of society can only be achieved by individual contributions irrespective of how small these efforts are. The heart does not care about race, religion, looks, age, or distance, but all it knows is how the other person makes you feel."

Ultimately, my mission is to emphasize brotherhood, peace, and unity as we look to better our own future, the future of our community, and Nigeria at large. Therefore, my focus has always been on doing the little I can with a great love, sincerity, transparency, and honesty. My journey to help people to have a good life has always been my priority, and the foundation is the pinnacle of my achievement in this respect. It gives me great pride to look back on what it has achieved in only a few years.

CHAPTER 9

New Frontiers

e have accomplished a lot at Amaecom and at the Marcel Ofomata Foundation in our short years, but, never one to rest on my laurels, I devised even bigger ideas for the future: a foray into a new frontier in digital solutions.

Across the world, the consensus has been that developing nations need alternative sources of funding to complement the deficiencies in the banking sector. The answer for Nigeria, Ghana, and Cameroon was to offer leasing and asset financing, and this is how I bridged that gap. In only twelve years, I accomplished my goal to be the leading global grassroots one-stop asset financing company in Africa, and I did this by imbuing my company and foundation with my own core values of quality, integrity, and passion as well as transparency and inclusion. My business has been successful and delivered excellence. It continues to be transparent and have a strong desire to satisfy customers' needs as the core value.

Looking back, I saw that I accomplished what I set out to do:

enhance quality of life through the provision of unbeatable, stress-free asset acquisition solutions. Amaecom was the vanguard for this transformation in the lives of ordinary Nigerians. Not only did we provide workers with the means to acquire assets they needed over time, we offered transparent financing and helped them manage their cash-flow challenges by becoming part of our trusted asset financing system.

When we started back in 2004 as a nonbank financial institution providing asset financing solutions and asset management services, I used my own equity to get started and reinvested in the company to expand from one office to thirty in Nigeria, and others in Cameroon, Ghana, and China. To help this expansion I went back to school, training at MIT and Harvard.

Over the years, we had perfected the process of BuyNow PayLater™ to give families access to assets they needed without having the funds available. We were able to make their dreams happen while maintaining risk management and operational excellence. We have truly come a long way.

Many years ago, I set out with little more than passion and integrity to try to fill the gaps in people's lives and make a significant difference. This focus on people before profit, ironically, was the very value that allowed us to remain profitable while our competitors were going out of business. I have said a number of times in this book that I believed our success was due to innovation and to holding fast to our core values in a market where competitors were often less than transparent. Authenticity has been key in our growth. It has engendered trust both in the government and in our clients for the products and services we offer.

I also took a unique approach to business. I always saw business as a partnership, not only with my manufacturing partners, but also with my employees and our customers. Across the board, my staff and

I focused on training, branding, and quality to deliver high performance results.

We also looked to Nigeria as a whole and took pride in the strength of our diversity. It wasn't always easy to diversify. It may have been less expensive to hire people indigenous to the local office instead of incurring the expense of relocating people to other tribal regions, but it

> **I ALWAYS SAW BUSINESS AS A PARTNERSHIP, NOT ONLY WITH MY MANUFACTURING PARTNERS, BUT ALSO WITH MY EMPLOYEES AND OUR CUSTOMERS.**

was important to me as a businessman to contribute to a stable, united, and prosperous Nigeria. Thankfully, those early experiences living with my aunt were invaluable in this respect and paid off handsomely, both financially and culturally, in later years.

Nevertheless, I have even more great ambitions to improve efficiency, customer relevance, and profitability to continue to grow our company.

A New Five-Year Plan

Having come this far, we devised a new five-year plan to expand from over fifty thousand customers currently to one million. As Andre Gide asserts, "Man cannot discover new oceans unless he has the courage to lose sight of the shore." It's an ambitious plan. However, as Africa's largest market, Nigerian asset financing has experienced an average of double-digit growth over the last decade, despite still being in its infancy stage with a low penetration rate. To lead this transition we had the privilege of signing on Professor Ndubuisi Ekekwe (MBA, PhD) of Famiscro Group.

The banks continue to play a dominant role in providing funds to lessors at the high end of the market, where they finance big-ticket leases. However, nonbank lessors today contribute to 80 percent of lease transactions in terms of customer base, concentrating mainly on the middle-to-lower-end market.

Over the past few years, investors have taken Nigeria's middle-to-lower-end asset financing and leading market by storm. Total investment in the sector is projected to hit $5 billion by 2023. This is being helped by the standardization of citizen identification to enable mass consumer-level asset financing. To achieve this standardization, we are moving into a more technology-driven organizational structure so that we can rapidly access data and do instant risk assessment. This approach to business has served us well in the past and will continue to do so in the future.

To accomplish this growth we want to see in our customer base, we are moving beyond the government employee sector into the private sector. We have traditionally focused on the public sector, financing the acquisition of assets for mainly government employees at both state and federal levels.

In 2003, we started offering instant loans to existing private and public sector clients who are creditworthy. Now we have plans to work with trade associations and cooperatives to continue to provide access to finance to acquire assets that improve the quality of lives of public sector workers in our BuyNow PayLater™ plan. Soon, we will expand this to private-sector workers.

We are also planning to offer instant loans and seed capital to small entrepreneurs. Branching into small to medium enterprises (SMEs) financing and consumer asset financing is the next logical step in our growth. Not only will it expand our unique approach to nonbanking financing, it will create employment, reduce poverty, and make our company more sustainable than ever. I am confident as we embark on this new venture that we will be as successful in it as we have been in everything else we've tackled along the way.

We can offer financing for vehicles, motorcycles, computers, and any other product. Not only does this allow the customer to treat their asset as a tax-deductible operating expense, it allows us to improve our balance sheet because of the assets we have on the books, and it gives us better lines of credit and cash flow.

Of course, to offer this financing structure without compromising our strong risk-management policy, we need instant access to credit history, employment records, and other background information on our potential clients. The widespread use of standard citizen identification systems in Nigeria is an essential resource, which will allow us assess our risk as we move forward. To do this efficiently, we are planning to invest in technology that will allow us to become more agile.

Nigeria is primed for technology-driven operations. Information and communication technology (ICT) is rapidly moving the country toward knowledge-based economic structures and information societies, and this is what will allow us expand and reach my new goal to increase our customer base to one million customers over the next five years.

It may sound ambitious for a little enterprise that started out in a tiny shop in Eket, and it may sound like a lot of customers, but bear in mind that Nigeria is Africa's largest economy with over 180 million people and GDP of $405 billion.[13] The population has quadrupled over the last five decades, with 62 percent under the age of twenty-four, and is projected to grow to 392 million in 2050.[14] The

---

13   "Nigeria GDP," *Trading Economic*, accessed November 2018, https://tradingeconomics.com/nigeria/gdp

14   "The World Factbook: Nigeria," Central Intelligence Agency, accessed November 2018, https://www.cia.gov/library/publications/the-world-factbook/geos/ni.html

nation is experiencing rapid urbanization, with 49.8 percent of total population currently in cities, as the economy moves from mainly agrarian base to a more service-oriented sector. Nigeria is also experiencing an expanding middle class, which makes it poised for growth in finance, energy, telecommunications, entertainment, and indeed all key sectors of modern commerce and industry. It is important to harness the potential of this burgeoning population in order to boost economic development.

From Strength to Success

We are in a good position to manifest our plan to reach one million customers. The Marcel Ofomata Foundation plans to continue to offer scholarships and mentorships to talented entrepreneurs to steer youth into productive activities. Amaecom is also doing its part to boost economic development, offer employment to help reduce poverty, and contribute to an acceptable standard of living in Nigeria. We plan to continue or core value of diversity so that we will continue to be a role model in Nigerian leadership that is leading youths away from religious or ethnic violence. Because Amaecom has strong leadership capabilities and branches in strategic cities and access to public sector trade associations as well as governmental decision makers, I anticipate we will be able to continue to not only contribute to the prosperity of the "Giant of Africa" as we have always done but to increase our market share.

After our years of work to perfect our financing plan and build our own manufacturing processes, we have a strong and identifiable brand name, strong technology capabilities, an understanding of the Nigerian market both tapped and untapped, an optimized cost structure, and an edge on the competition. We also have a highly trained and loyal workforce, and a potential partnership with M&M Business School, which will allow us to expand capacity and train enough people to support our one million customers. All in all, we have new huge scalable advantages to make our latest target achievable.

It has been an exciting journey since I first started out with only a few naira in my pocket. To witness the transformation of Nigeria as I have done over the years and the potential inherent in Africa Rising promises to be an exciting few decades ahead as we continue to grow, partner, innovate, encourage young entrepreneurs, attract foreign investors, and above all keep our focus on needs of the people.

This new venture into technology and into our new phase to reach one million customers brings my story that started in one little corner of Africa up to date and promises to lead us into exciting and expansive years ahead.

CHAPTER 10

A Final Word

hen I made the decision to write this book, I did so because the success story of Nigeria has been downplayed. People hear of civil war and political upheaval or nepotism, but people have not had the benefit of hearing the story of how innovative and enterprising Nigerians are and how buoyant the economy has become. We rarely hear about the "Giant of Africa" in a progressive and entrepreneurial sense.

Young Nigerians need inspiration, and this is what I intend to provide them by showing them what is possible. I wanted to show that there are people who believe in this country working quietly and successfully here. For non-Nigerians reading this book, I wanted to show what a great country this is and why you should come here, live and work here, and invest here. For all readers, I have attempted to show that there is a lot of opportunity here and that there are people in their own space doing what they can. I also want to instill this knowledge in the youth in Nigeria because this attitude should be encouraged.

If people are open to learning and are willing to work, then they can make so much of their lives here. As Joy Bell asserts, "The only person who can pull me down is myself, and I'm not going to let myself pull me down anymore." They can make a real impact. I see people go to the US to work and they don't make the impact one businessman with good values can make here. Today, there are still many areas waiting for someone with vision and transparency to make a mark the way I have done in my own small way.

I hope my book will make people share the pride I have in Nigeria. I hope it will encourage people to invest in our economy and in my company. I hope people will believe in our brand and be inspired by our goals to leave a legacy of quality, respect, and authenticity.

Writing this book for me has been rewarding. It has given me great pride to reflect back on my years, the wonderful people I met, and the services we've been able to provide. I'm also proud of our ability to scale up and grow in order to both meet people's needs and know that the company will continue to do this after I'm gone. I'm also proud that we figured this out as we went. No one at Amaecom started with the skills we now have as a company and as a culture, but building our culture based on our values has allowed us be authentic and faithful to them through the years.

I started out with the aim to be successful by adding value to people's lives. My instinct that business would flourish on that basis was right. I believe in the power of giving. I believe that when you give, you never lack. When I say giving, I don't mean arbitrarily. I have never fostered dependency by offering handouts; all the ways I gave have been to empower people to improve their lives. I know that since I started giving, I have been greatly rewarded and have never lacked.

Another personal core value is my love of Nigeria, and I have been blessed that I have been able to bring this into my company by championing diversity in the workplace and finding strength in that diversity. Even when I was starting out in Uyo with very little to my name, I was as fair as I could be. When I got on my feet, I offered a good wage to reflect the demands of the various positions in my company. Some other companies didn't do that. I did because I wanted my staff to know they are valuable, just as my customers are valuable.

At the end of the day, a business has to make money, but there are ways to do that while being ethical. I'm proud to say that we have done that; even in our darkest hour, we put people first. It paid off because

EVEN IN OUR DARKEST HOUR, WE PUT PEOPLE FIRST.

today I have a terrific team. Teamwork—aligning everybody to the vision—has been of great importance and has helped us get to where we are today.

Four Valuable Life Lessons

When I look back over my life, from the earliest days when I was cutting palm leaves for my mother, I realize how fortunate I have been to have had invaluable learning experiences along the way. If I were to assess the most important and impactful lessons or experiences in my life, I'd have to say simply having a good, positive attitude to life and loving the people around me has offered me great learning experiences. I learned that when I believe in other people, it shows in the way I communicate with them, the choice of words I use, and how I deliver them. That belief comes back tenfold and propels us all to great success. After all, success without people is meaningless. People have helped me all along the way, and I have tried my best to help them and continue to do so. In all the change I have experienced over the years, one thing that has never changed is my respect for other people.

The second most valuable experience relates to my failures. I have failed, many times. Each time, I was fearful because I didn't want to fail again, but some of the most invaluable lessons I have learned were through my failures. One thing I learned back in my days in a motorcycle shop in Eket was to assume the deal would be a disaster or there would be trouble and have a contract in place first. Failures can be powerful learning experiences.

The third relates to my thirst for learning. This can drive you. I always wanted to learn. Every time I travel, I learn something new. I'm an eternal student. I'm smart enough to know that other people know better than me; they always know something better. When I was ten and twelve, even twenty, I spent my time with people in their forties, fifties, and sixties to learn from their wisdom and experience. Now as a man in his forties, I spend time with people in their twenties and thirties because they have energy and drive. The wisdom of the elderly and the strength of the young are important for success.

For the individuals hoping to succeed in business here today, I say first remember that your background, that is, where you were born or how you were raised, does not determine the heights you can reach in life. You can be anything you want to be. That is very important to know. Remember, see failures as positives because every failure you have teaches you something new. Never be afraid to take a risk because you're afraid to fail. Finally, have the thirst for learning. This is key.

If you, the reader, take away only one point from this whole book, I hope it is the importance of being authentic. We succeeded in business and in serving humanity because we here at Amaecom in Nigeria are authentic and real. We are profitable, and we are beautiful, wonderful people to work with. Nigeria is filled with the best people on earth.

ABOUT THE AUTHOR

Dr. Amaechi Ofomata is a visionary leader, entrepreneur, mentor, and philanthropist both in his home country of Nigeria and around the world. His leadership approach is built on a powerful yet simple philosophy that businesses flourish when they add true value to the lives of other people.

Today, Dr. Ofomata has over fifteen years of practical entrepreneurship, managerial leadership, and mentorship experience. He is currently the founder and CEO of Africa's leading asset financing company, Amaecom Global Limited, which has branches in Nigeria, Cameroon, Ghana, and China. Its trademarked BuyNow PayLater™ model of asset acquisition has transformed the lives of thousands of ordinary Nigerians. In 2018, Amaecom was named as one of Nigeria's top fifty professional brands.

Over the years, he has led Amaecom Global Limited from idea to significance, from a start-up to Africa's leading asset financing company. Having known hunger and deprivation and been exposed to less-than-scrupulous businessmen in his formative years, he adopted three core values that underpin all his business dealings and philanthropic ventures: quality (distinguishing character of excellence), integrity (transparent and equitable manner), and passion (strong desire to satisfy).

Through innovation and foresight, Amaecom is now one of Africa's most award-winning enterprises. With staff spread across Nigeria, Cameroon, Ghana, and China, the company's engineering, global manufacturing, services, and product development expertise has set a high standard for what an indigenous company can aim for and achieve.

Dr. Ofomata's emphasis on vision, transparency, authenticity, and meeting the needs of the people has been further exemplified through the establishment of Nigeria's first practice-based, hands-on business school. The Mitchell & Michelle (M&M) Business School is an innovator in education that challenges the standard education delivery model in Africa. The M&M school focuses on producing industry-ready graduates with proven competence and skills relevant to today's emerging Africa.

With the goal of contributing to the development of indigenous manufacturing, Amaechi established the first high-technology-run mattress/furniture production industry in Akwa Ibom State. This has been a giant stride in diversifying the nation's economy and bringing it into alignment with the industrialization policy of the state and federal governments.

In 2013, Dr. Ofomata founded the Marcel Ofomata Foundation to meet the needs of education and mentorship in Nigeria. It offers grants and mentorships to underprivileged but talented young entrepreneurs. It helps them achieve success in business and industry and instills in them the fundamental principle of giving back.

Dr. Ofomata is learning chairman of the prestigious Entrepreneurs Organization (EO), Abuja Chapter. He is an alumnus of Harvard Business School, Massachusetts Institute of Technology, and Abia State University, where he obtained a bachelor's degree in accounting.

Dr. Ofomata is also a member of the Chartered Institute of Leadership and the Institute of Chartered Economists of Nigeria. He has earned Paul Harris Fellow recognition for contributions to the Rotary Foundation's ambassadorial scholarships. He is a grand patron of Nigerian Red Cross, a Justice of Peace, and a Jerusalem Pilgrim. He has received over 102 awards from international, national, state, and grassroots organizations and holds the chieftaincy titles of Onwa Isuofia in Igbo land and Obong Unwan in Akwa Ibom State and Akpa' K'Idoma of Idoma Kingdom in North Central Nigeria.

He lives in Abuja, Nigeria, with his wife, Chika, and two sons and two daughters. In his spare time, he enjoys a round of golf.

DR. AMAECHI OFOMATA
Amaecom Global Ltd
NAF Valley Asokoro
+234 80 278 9699
Abuja, Nigeria
marcel.o@amaecomglobal.com

APPENDIX

AMAECHI OFOMATA
Founder, Amaecom Global Limited

SUMMARY
Visionary leader, entrepreneur, and mentor, Amaechi Ofomata has led Amaecom Global Limited from idea to significance, from start-up to Africa's leading asset financing company. Through innovation and foresight, he has been able to position the company as one of Africa's leading enterprises. With staff spread across Nigeria, Cameroon, Ghana, and China, the company's engineering, global manufacturing, and services and product development expertise has set a high standard for what an indigenous company can aim for and achieve. Amaechi Ofomata's leadership approach is built on a powerful yet simple philosophy that businesses flourish when they add true value to the lives of people. This has led to the establishment of other subsidiaries under the Amaecom group of companies including Amaecom Trading Company, Amaecom Foam and Furniture Manufacturing,

and the Marcel Ofomata Foundation, to name a few.

Amaechi's philosophy was further exemplified through the establishment of Nigeria's first practice-based, hands-on business school, the Mitchell & Michelle Business School, an innovation in education that challenges the status quo of the standard education delivery model in Africa. It focuses on content and curriculum on churning out industry-ready graduates with proven competence and skills relevant to today's emerging Africa. By establishing the first high-technology-run mattress/furniture production facility in Akwa, Ibom State, Amaechi made a giant leap in diversifying the nation's economy into industrialization, which is consistent with the policy of Nigerian state and federal governments.

EXPERIENCE

Founding President
Mitchell & Michelle Business School
January 2015–Present

Learning Chair
Entrepreneurs' Organization
September 2018–Present

Founding Director
Marcel Ofomata Foundation
January 2014–Present

Founder
Amaecom Global Ltd.
April 2004–Present

President
Entrepreneur's Organization
June 2017–July 2018

Relationship Partner
Standard Trust Bank
January 2003–March 2004

EDUCATION

Massachusetts Institute of Technology
MA Entrepreneurship/Entrepreneurial Studies
2017–2019

Harvard Business School
Certificate Business Administration and Management
2013

Abia State University
Bachelor of Science (BS) in Accounting
1994–1999

HONORS AND AWARDS

FCIL, PHF, MD+1, ICEN
"Onwa" of the Ancient Kingdoms of Isuofia, Anambra State
"Akpa K'Idoma"
Idoma Land, Benue State
"Obong Unwan"
Akwa, Ibom State

TRAININGS UNDERGONE AND CERTIFICATES ACQUIRED

EO New York Global University
The Entrepreneurs' Organization
New York, 2015

One Level Up Training
The Entrepreneurs' Organization
Munich, 2016

Moderator Training in Conjunction with Middle East, Asia, and Africa
The Entrepreneurs' Organization
Cape Town, 2017

Creating a More Prosperous Commonwealth
Commonwealth Business Forum
Malta, 2017

Global Leadership Conference
The Entrepreneurs' Organization
Frankfurt, 2017

Mexico Global University
The Entrepreneurs' Organization
Mexico, 2017

Foundation for Growth
Entrepreneurs' Organization Grow
Dubai, 2018

President Meeting cum Training
Europe, Middle East, Pakistan, and Africa
Greece, 2018

Global Leadership Academy

The Entrepreneurs' Organization
Washington, DC, 2018

Asia Bridge Forum Training
Cambodia, 2018

Global Leadership Conference
The Entrepreneurs' Organization
Toronto, 2018

MYEO Deal Exchange Conference
The Entrepreneurs' Organization
Denver, 2018

Social Impact Business Summit
The Entrepreneurs' Organization
Sri Lanka, 2019

Entrepreneurial Master's Program
Massachusetts Institute of Technology
Massachusetts, 2019

Global Leadership Conference
The Entrepreneurs' Organization
Macau, 2019

Asia Bridge Forum
Malaysia, 2019

CHILDHOOD PHOTOS

My first communion, Isuofia

Dressed in Calabar royal attire at the age of fifteen, Eket

The first picture taken upon my arrival in Eket